Trust and Obey

Trust and Obey

Pleasing Christ While Avoiding Legalism and Lawlessness

OLAN STUBBS

Foreword by Brandon Crowe

WIPF & STOCK · Eugene, Oregon

TRUST AND OBEY
Pleasing Christ While Avoiding Legalism and Lawlessness

Wipf & Stock
An Imprint of Wipf and Stock Publishers
199 W. 8th Ave., Suite 3
Eugene, OR 97401

www.wipfandstock.com

PAPERBACK ISBN: 979-8-3852-7056-9
HARDCOVER ISBN: 979-8-3852-7057-6
EBOOK ISBN: 979-8-3852-7058-3

VERSION NUMBER 021226

This book is dedicated to two of my former pastors, Frank Barker and Harry Reeder, who greatly helped me understand and apply covenant and reformed theology.

Contents

Foreword

Brandon Crowe

Our age is one of much confusion. We are bombarded with the worldly message that freedom comes by following our own desires. Some of the mantras are well-known:

"You do you."

"Follow your heart."

"Be true to yourself."

These self-centered bromides do not reflect a scriptural worldview, but they instead exalt the feelings and whims of the individual to the place of moral arbiter. This manner of thinking seems to leave little to no space for the input of God's law. In such thinking, the law of God—if it is considered at all—is perhaps seen as restrictive and confining. It is something to be avoided or rejected, not something to be delighted in.

But our age is not unique in this mindset. The human heart is the same today as it was in biblical times. Sinners naturally rebel against God's law, even though it is ingrained in creation. No one can actually escape God's law. We are all created in God's image and innately know something about who God is and what he requires of us. And yet sin makes us foolish and leads us to reject the will of our Creator. This is not to our benefit, but to our great detriment.

We need to recover the role and goodness of God's law today.

Scripture teaches us the right way to think about God's law. The psalmist speaks of the blessing for the one who delights in God's law (Ps 1:2). The law is a lamp to our feet and a light to our path (Ps 119:105). Jesus teaches us that the two greatest commandments are love for God and love for neighbor (Matt 22:37–39). James even talks about the law of freedom (Jas 1:25).

Some may reject God's law altogether; that view needs correcting. Others may agree in theory that God's law is good, but have a hard time knowing how in practice to love God's law. Doesn't God's law show us our sinfulness? How can we be expected to obey God's law when we're sinners? Isn't that impossible? What about the hypocrites in the church?

That is why I'm thankful for this new book from my friend Olan Stubbs. He knows how to communicate, and in this book he teaches readers about the importance of God's law throughout Scripture. He also explains how the law relates to us today. He shows how the law is good, but also how the law can be misused.

On the one hand, we need to understand that no sinner can keep the law of God faithfully enough to merit God's favor. That is legalism. On the other hand, we need to understand that rejecting the law of God (antinomianism) is also a grave error.

This book will help you understand how to understand the goodness of God's law in the context of the goodness of God's covenants with his people.

There's much more here as well that will be useful. Understanding the role of the law can help us understand the grand narrative of the entire Bible. How do we understand Adam's role in the beginning? This is a foundational question. Were people saved by works under in the Old Testament? (Spoiler alert: no!) How does the gospel message relate to our ongoing need to obey God's law? This book will help you answer all these questions, and will do so in language that is not overly technical. Trying to understand the law of God can be a complex process, but this book will provide sure guidance through the morass.

And this book will also help you see how the law of God points us to Christ himself. Our hope is ultimately not in the law or in our ability to keep the law. But our hope must be in what Christ has done in our stead.

What does that mean?

Take up and read!

Preface

What is the moral law of God? How does God's law interact with God's covenants with mankind? Is the moral law still applicable today? How does it apply to Christians who've been saved by grace alone, through faith alone, not by works of the law? Do I still have to obey the Bible? What about the Old Testament? There's some weird stuff in there; should I obey it all?

Maybe you've asked or wondered about some of the previous questions. They are very important questions. Unfortunately, many Christians struggle with knowing the right answers to one or more of the above questions. In the middle of that doubt and fog, deeper problems can arise.

All people, including mature Christians, either struggle with legalism or licentiousness. We will define both terms in more detail as we go, but a simple explanation will suffice for now.[1] A legalist would seem to treat the law of God too seriously in some respects. There would be some legal aspect of their personal relationship with God. "If I don't keep all these commandments just right, there's no way God can truly bless me! Is there?" This might be a fear they struggle with.

On the other hand, many others would struggle with being a libertine. They would throw off all constraints. "Well, if I'm saved by grace, and not by works, let the party begin! I can get drunk, get high, sleep around, and chase money in this life as much as I want. I'll have the best this life has to offer, all the sinful pleasures I can handle. All my sins, past, present, and future are forgiven. So, let's relax and enjoy, for Jesus paid it all. We can have our cake in this sinful life and eat it too, sinless in heaven in the next life. All is well."

1. I will use the terms "lawless," "libertine," "licentious," and "antinomian" as essentially synonymous throughout this book. There's a glossary at the end of the book that explains some of the terms you may not be familiar with.

Both are extreme examples. There are more subtle ways we can fall into these traps. But Christians should desire to thread the needle between these two ditches. This is why I've written this book.

To properly understand the place of the moral law in our lives as Christians, it is very helpful to understand some things about the Biblical covenants. We don't have to be an expert on covenant theology to obey God's moral law. This book will say virtually nothing about God's covenant with Noah and David for example. But we will dive deep into God's covenant with Adam, Abraham, and more. The goal is to understand enough about how the covenants function to be able to understand how God's moral law functions in them.

I want to help believers understand the proper role and balance of the moral law of God in their day-to-day life. How serious should they take it? What place should they give it? How can we live fully in grace and yet be passionate and serious about personal holiness. The Bible tells us how. Join me on this journey.

There are some sermons that go along with this book.[2] I also use some stories in this book to help make the principles clear and applicable. Some details of some stories have been changed to protect anonymity.

2. Stubbs, "Law and Covenant."

Acknowledgments

I WANT TO THANK Wipf and Stock for working with me again. I want to thank my wife for supporting me in this work. Mostly I thank Christ for saving me and leading me in his truth.

Chapter 1

Adamic Covenant

THE WORD "COVENANT" NEVER shows up in the first three chapters of the Bible, but the concept does. This is a massive biblical concept. It is extremely helpful in understanding how human beings interact with and relate with their creator. Hosea 6:7 does say, "But like Adam they have transgressed the covenant." God made a covenant with Adam in Gen 2, though the specific word is not used.

My layman's definition of a biblical covenant is "a solemn relationship with conditions and consequences," or "a unilateral oath with implications." By unilateral I mean that one person establishes the relationship with the other. God brought us into relationship with him as his creatures whether we wanted to be made or not. God's covenants are not negotiated relationships where we bargain with God for a better deal. There may not be conditions for us to meet to get into the covenant. But there are always massive implications. At its essence, a covenant is a relationship. But it is more than that.

Imagine you went out to eat today. The server introduced himself as Bill. You had never met before, but you chatted for a moment, ordered your food, ate, paid the bill, and said "Goodbye, Bill." You might technically say you have a relationship with Bill in the most basic sense. You don't have a covenant relationship with Bill though. You are under no obligation to go back to see Bill or talk to Bill or order food from Bill again. If you totally forget about Bill, there will be no obvious consequences. That's not the way a covenant works.

We rarely use the word "covenant" today. But if we do, what's the context that comes to mind? Most would say marriage, though some might say a homeowner's association. Marriage is the most intense relationship you can have with another human being. Legal documents must be signed. To break it, the law is involved again. Marriage is a solemn relationship. It is a serious relationship. Even a homeowner's agreement tends to have some teeth. You are making certain promises and can be held accountable for them. There can be consequences if you don't live up to your word.

Marriages come with conditions. We tend to take vows. Even signing legal documents to get married in the presence of a notary public is a condition of sorts. Marriage certainly brings consequences. If both parties do it right, there may be many wonderful blessings and joys that result. If one or both parties don't treat the relationship seriously, painful consequences can ensue.

Covenant

Let's see how this covenant plays out in the Garden of Eden with Adam. Different Bible teachers will sometimes refer to this covenant as the covenant of life, of law, or of works. In the 1600s some of the greatest Bible teachers of all time gathered in England to write a summary of the Bible's teachings called the Westminster Confession of Faith and Catechism.[1] I'll refer to both throughout this book.

The Westminster Shorter Catechism (WSC) question 12 is answered, "God . . . entered into a covenant of life with him, on condition of perfect obedience, forbidding him to eat of the tree of the knowledge of good and evil on penalty of death."[2] Westminster Confession of Faith (WCF) 7.2 says, "The first covenant made with humanity was a covenant of works. In it life was promised to Adam and, in him, to his descendants, on condition of perfect and personal obedience." WCF 19.1 says, "God gave to Adam a law in the form of a covenant of works, by which he bound him and all his posterity to personal, complete, exact, and perpetual obedience. God promised life if Adam kept the law and threatened death if he broke it, and gave him power and ability to keep it." The essence of this first covenant was "Do this and you will live." See Lev 18:5 for an example.

1. The Westminster Confession of Faith and the Larger and Shorter Catechism (essentially a question-and-answer teaching format) were developed by English and Scottish theologians from 1643–1647 as a statement of what the Bible teaches

2. All quotes from the Westminster Confession of Faith and Catechism will be taken from *The Westminster Confession and Catechisms in Modern English*, edited by Rowald S. Ward.

Genesis 1 tells the story of God making all things. God is making a world for man to inhabit. On the sixth day, the story slows down and focuses. God seems to confer with himself, saying, "Let Us make man in Our image, according to Our likeness" (Gen 1:26). This does not give us the full-blown doctrine of the Trinity, but it certainly paves the way for it.

The Bible teaches there is one God who exists eternally in three persons. These three persons have lived in loving relationship with one another forever. They know and enjoy one another.

God decided to make people in his own image, his reflection, his likeness. God the three in one had been having eternal fellowship together. He decided to make humans that they would join and enjoy the fellowship. We would not be gods, but we would share relationship with him.

God did not create people because he was weak, lonely, or needy. He created us out of joy, fullness, and overflow. He wanted to enjoy us, and he wanted us to delight in him as well. WSC 1 says, "The chief purpose for which man was made is to glorify God, and to enjoy him forever."

Adam, the first man, later had "a son in his own likeness, according to his image" (Gen 5:3). This is a very similar phrase as we see in Gen 1:26. "Likeness" and "image" is family language. People today might see a man who favors his father physically and say, "He's the spitting image of his daddy." In a similar fashion, all humans are made in the image of God. Paul teaches that all people are "the offspring of God" (Acts 17:29). What exactly does this mean? God had no physical body at this time. So, the implication in Gen 1:26 is not that the first man and woman will look physically like God. But in other ways we were made very similar to God.

Human beings were made to have a deep, personal, spiritual relationship with God, their creator. The main way that humans and animals are different is humans have capacity to know and enjoy God. We were made for fellowship with the Divine.

Dolphins may be smart. Orangutans may do some things that seem "humanlike." But you'll never find a group of apes or monkeys or parakeets anywhere sitting around reading a book about their relationship with God and wondering exactly what that means. They don't have that capacity. They aren't made in his image.

On the first five days of creation, at the end of the day, "God saw that it was good" (Gen 1:21). His world looked right, beautiful, symmetrical, fruitful, purposeful, just as he had designed it. But on the sixth day, after humans were made, "it was very good" (Gen 1:31). Once humans were brought into this wonderful world God had designed for them, God's pleasure in his creation was even greater and fuller. God delights in sunsets and ocean breezes. But he takes greater delight in men and women who know him, love him, trust him, and interact with him.

Genesis 2:2 tells us that God rested on the seventh day. But "the Creator of the ends of the earth / Does not become weary or tired" (Isa 40:28). So why did God rest?

This is the rest of enjoyment. Imagine your favorite pastime is cutting your grass or weeding your flower bed or washing your car. It does not exhaust you at all. Rather, it exhilarates you and gives you life. Maybe painting a picture gives you such satisfaction. Imagine being done, grabbing your favorite beverage, sitting down, leaning back, looking at what your hands have just done and smiling with joy and pleasure. You enjoy the finished work. It's beautiful, noteworthy, and delightful to you. That's how God felt on day seven. He made a world perfectly fit for man to grow and thrive. He sat back so to speak, smiled, and enjoyed his work.

Many people read Gen 1–2 and want to spend endless hours in debate over dinosaurs, the age of the earth, and evolution. I'm not saying there is no point in that. I am saying that's not the main point. The main point is God made everything. And God made everything for his glory but also for the enjoyment and blessing of his people. God made a glorious world, a relational world, a very inhabitable world. Please don't miss this most important point. He made a world fit for mankind.

Augustine, one of the greatest theologians of all time, says,

> Shall I speak of the manifold and various loveliness of sky, and earth, and sea; of the plentiful supply and wonderful qualities of the light; of sun, moon, and stars; of the shade of trees; of the colours and perfume of flowers; of the multitude of birds, all differing in plumage and in song . . . ? What shall I say of the numberless kinds of food to alleviate hunger, and the variety of seasonings to stimulate appetite which are scattered everywhere by nature, and for which we are not indebted to the art of cookery? How many natural appliances are there for preserving and restoring health! How grateful is the alteration of day and night! How pleasant the breezes that cool the air! How abundant the supply of clothing furnished us by trees and animals! Who can enumerate all the blessings we enjoy?[3]

3. Augustine, *City of God*, 854.

We should always be shocked and amazed at Father God's lavish and generous provision for us in this world!

God loves to give good gifts to his children. One reason many people prefer to call this first covenant the covenant of life is that it feels wrong to call it a covenant of works. It feels wrong because Adam didn't start from a place of neutrality. Adam didn't start at zero with a command to work his way to 100 percent fullness. Rather he started in a very blessed place. He started already experiencing much grace, goodness, and kindness. He started from a wonderful and easy place, the garden of Eden.

Conditions

But many still prefer to call this first covenant with man the covenant of works. Because there was work to be done. There were conditions to be met. This was not to be a creation or relationship of passivity but one of glorious activity. God set the pattern for us. Work six days, rest one.

God is a worker. He is a creator, a cultivator, a developer. If we are to reflect his goodness and glory (which he intends us to do), then we must do the things God does. We cannot create out of nothing like he can. We can take the raw materials that he gives us in a tree and make shelter though. We were made to be God's second-in-command on planet earth. He delegates many duties to us. He gives us important tasks to do, not merely busy work.

Genesis 1:26 teaches that we are supposed to rule over all the animals. Genesis 1:28 teaches that we are supposed to have babies and multiply humanity. We are supposed to subdue the earth and cover it with little living statues of God, so to speak.

Kings in the ancient near east would show their dominion over a certain territory by placing statues of themselves throughout their kingdoms. A similar practice is done today when the face of the ruler is printed on money that is used throughout a country. God wants all of planet earth covered with living images of him.

God has given us all we need to live a wonderful life on planet earth. He has given us food, land, sunlight, warmth, rest, and friends. He has thought of everything. He has given us the mind, ability, and capacity to rule the earth well, to develop it even further as a welcome place to live.

You could say that the vows of the Adamic covenant were God saying to Adam, "I'll satisfy you and you'll serve me." God made this covenant with Adam in the garden. It was a great deal. Work at this time was all blessing and no thorns. There was no hardship, pain, or monotony in serving God in Eden.

Genesis 2 tells us that God made a garden and put Adam into it to work it. He told him that he could eat abundantly from all the trees in the garden save one. "From any tree of the garden you may eat freely" (Gen 2:16). In Hebrew one way to emphasize a word or concept is to repeat it. In Hebrew the phrase would read "eat, eat," meaning "eat freely." Eat your heart out, we might say. Eat until your heart is fully content. It could be translated, "Devour, devour!" Enjoy yourself, eat freely and fully. Have a perpetual feast.

There is one tree they were not allowed to eat from. But before God ever gave one prohibition, he gave a lifetime of freedom. Before one "no" he gave a very kind and gracious "yes" to eat from any other tree of the garden. Don't forget the generosity of God.

We are never told exactly why they could not eat from the one tree. There is no indication that it was poisonous. The implication more seems to be that it was a test for Adam. Thousands of years later we can be tempted or bothered by this. Why did God do this? Was he setting Adam up for a fall? Is it fair? Was it the best and wisest thing to do?

God seems to be saying, "Adam, you get the privilege to live in this glorious and wonderful relationship with me, your Creator. You will get many high privileges. You are my vice-regent (my right-hand man). I am delegating to you much power, prestige, and authority, and even independence in a sense. But never forget, I'm God and you're not. I'm the master and the leader. You are the servant and the follower."

The one prohibited tree made this point very well. The implication is, "Trust me. You don't have to know why. Just know that I know best. Obey me for that is always for your best. I want to help, not hinder you. I always aim to bless and not unnecessarily burden you. Obey me, just because I told you so and because you love and trust me."

God is all wise and all-knowing and he knows that when we are very blessed, the blessing can go to our heads. We can become intoxicated with the goodness of God in a way that hurts us. When he blesses us so richly there is a tendency for those blessings to sinfully go to our heads. Deuteronomy 6 contains a warning for God's people in the wilderness. God tells them that he will bring them into the promised land and give them houses, lands, wealth, and more. But he warns, "Watch yourself, lest you forget the LORD who brought you from the land of Egypt, out of the house of slavery" (Deut 6:12).

Adam was in a place of incredible blessing. Yet he had free will. He needed to willingly choose to humble himself, to stay humble, and to continually submit to God as Lord in obedience.

Immediately after the one prohibition God goes right back to blessing Adam more. The one "no" was bracketed by gracious "yeses." God invents woman, one of his greatest creations of all time. "Adam, take a nap buddy. And when you wake up, I've got a huge surprise for you!" God invented the marriage partnership and all that goes with it. God is a wonderful Father who loves to give amazing gifts to his kids.

You would think that Adam would have been so humbled, so grateful, and overwhelmed with awe at God's goodness and kindness that he would have spent a full year just thanking the Lord for inventing woman! Otherwise, all his days would have been spent hanging out with porcupines, humpback whales, bald eagles, and chimpanzees. These are amazing creatures but nothing like a best human friend.

Genesis 2 ends with the man and woman in a state of innocence. They have nothing to hide, nothing to fake, nothing to prove, nothing to lie about, nothing to fear, nothing to be embarrassed about. They are at home with themselves, with each other, and with God. They are comfortable in a very literal sense in their own skin.

They are free to experience deep intimacy with one another and with their Creator. This is what they and we are made for. This is what we long for. This is covenantal relationship and intimacy.

The implication seems to be that if man had obeyed for a long enough time (some type of probationary period) he would have eaten of the tree of life and been secured in a state of perpetual holiness without the possibility of sin. It seems this is what happened to the good angels who didn't rebel. How long might that probationary period have been? We don't know. But that didn't happen. They probably didn't last one day.

Consequences

In Gen 3, Satan, the fallen angel, comes into the garden in the guise of a serpent to deceive and thus drive a wedge between mankind and God. He wants to ruin this glorious relationship. Genesis 2:4–22 refers to God as the

"LORD God" eleven times. This is God's covenant name, Yahweh God. It is his personal name that emphasizes his loyalty to his people.

Satan merely calls God "God," never "LORD God." Satan acknowledges that God is powerful, that he is Creator. Satan does not acknowledge God as good, loving, wise, and a lavish provider for his people.

Satan focuses on God's law, God's rules, God's conditions. He tries to muddy the waters that were oh-so clear. Eve pushes back and fights well at first. But even as she responds she begins to overemphasize God's restrictive nature. "From the fruit of the tree which is in the middle of the garden, God has said, 'You shall not eat from it or touch it'" (Gen 3:3). Notice two things. She refers to God as merely God and not LORD God. Also, she says that God prohibited touching the fruit, which he had not. It is so subtle, and yet, it seems to be a slow and small step towards focusing on God's prohibition more than his provision. She didn't mention that fact that God said they could "devour, devour" from every other tree in the garden. She is quickly forgetting the liberality of God.

Then Satan attacks God's word again. He also attacks his trustworthiness and character. He essentially says, "Don't worry about God! His bark is worse than his bite. You're not going to die. Live a little! Get some forbidden fruit for yourself."

Maybe Satan can see her teetering at this point. Maybe she started to consider the temptation. Satan goes for the jugular. His last temptation is the worst and most deadly. "God's not good. He does not love you. He is not for you. He is an oppressor and tyrant trying to hold you back, keep you down, and restrict you from the best stuff in life. He is not gracious. He is too strict. He is out to get you, to hurt you, to hold you down, and to keep you from the best life. You can't trust him. To obey God is to hurt yourself. Break free. Provide for yourself!"

Is this not the same thought pattern that Satan, sin, and the sinful world culture whisper and shout to us constantly? Do you not see some of these evil tendencies in your evil heart even now? Think of our culture today, even inside of the church. Think of the parts of God's moral law we tend to doubt the most.

If two women really love one another romantically and they've been same-sex attracted their whole life and they're willing to live in monogamous marriage forever, can't they be married and be happy? In a heterosexual marriage, why does man get to be the head and the leader? Why does the wife have to submit to him? That's ridiculous! What if she's godlier or smarter or more accomplished? It's not fair! Husbands might ask, "Why do I have to cherish my wife even when she's mean to me and doesn't like or respect me or serve me?! I don't even know what 'cherish' means?!" Others might say, "Tithe?! Ten percent of all I earn for church, which is full of hypocrites anyway!? Are you serious? Have you seen the economy? I'm barely surviving out here!" And who of us has not at some point seriously questioned and/or wrestled the doctrine of eternal conscious suffering for all those who die without Christ? It seems too horrid to fully consider. Is it true?

Satan's temptations started thousands of years ago and are still strong today. Doubt God's word, wisdom, power, goodness, and love. Adam and Eve both listened, both ate, and both began to immediately experience the negative consequences of their fall from grace. The covenant curses came down hard and fast, just and true.

They experience shame before one another. Having been cut off from God's gracious presence, they try to fix the problem themselves with fig leaves. If they had been thinking rightly, they would have run to God, not away from him. They would have begged mercy and help from him rather than trying to piece together a solution apart from him. Not much has changed for humanity in this regard. We don't trust God so we think we must help and fix ourselves.

God comes in the garden looking for them. They are filled with fear and terror rather than joy and gladness. They run and hide.

God lovingly pursues them with questions. He is seeking to lure them to repentance. Yet they continue to verbally hide. They misdirect. They focus on the symptoms rather than the roots. "I was scared and felt naked," rather than "I sinned and am sorry." They blame-shift. "It's your fault and her fault!" "The devil made me do it!" They minimize. "Technically I guess I was there and had some small, seemingly insignificant role to play, but let's don't really focus on that just now."

Does any of this sound familiar? This is how most of us handle our own sin and conviction daily. Even if we are in Christ, we tend to still struggle with these old patterns of cover up.

Application

Either right now, or as soon as you finish this section or chapter, I invite you to put the book down for a few quiet moments. Spend a little focused time thinking honestly and earnestly about where you tend to doubt the goodness of God most in your life. Most of us, at first glance, may say something to the effect of, "I've got decent theology. I know God's good. I don't think God is evil." But probe deeper. Go below the surface. What do the fruits of your life say about your functional theology, not your written and spoken theology.

I led a men's Bible study one time on the topic of the goodness of God. I asked each man where they doubted God's goodness. A good friend of mine honestly said, "I really don't think I struggle with doubting the goodness of God."

At the end of the Bible study, we took prayer requests. This same friend said, "I have really struggled a lot with drunkenness lately and have given in a couple of times." I asked him, "Do you not see how that struggle is the outward evidence of an inward doubt of God's goodness towards you?"

My friend was a hard worker. At some level what his actions said he believed was "I work hard and come home exhausted. I need a little fun and relaxation in my life. I know drunkenness is sin. But God is not providing for my needs or desires in the best way. So, I must go outside of God's prescribed rules for some experience to satisfy myself."

Where are you doing that in life? Where are you divorcing God's law from his character? Where are you seeing God's rules for you not as a blessing but as a burden?

Though you may sing songs of God's grace and generosity, where do your actions say that you look at God's law with contempt? Where do you honestly think God is too restrictive in the basement of your heart? It may be small and subtle, but look hard. I promise it's there.

Once we begin to see the sinful doubt we must repent. We must ask God for mercy, which he is happy to give! Don't stop there. Ask him to change you and grow you. We should ask him to help us see all his words and law as good. We need to see even the restrictive parts of his law as a blessing for us. Even the hardest parts of his word are an extension of his goodness and love for us.

The story doesn't end with Adam and Eve's sin. Praise God that it doesn't. If it did, then we would be all doomed.

Conclusion

God did bring covenant curses that day. He started with Satan. But before God curses Adam and Eve, he blesses them in the curse he pronounces on Satan.

God promises Adam and Eve that they would not die fully that day. They would stay alive. They would have children. Satan wanted to win Adam and Eve to his team that day, but he lost. There would be war between Satan and humans from that day forward. One child of Adam and Eve would come one day and do battle with Satan in a very personal way. He would be tempted by Satan. He would be wounded by Satan. But he would ultimately crush Satan for good. He would defeat Satan and his lies forever.

Adam and Eve broke that law of the garden and thus deserved consequences. They did receive a curse that day but not directly. It was more of a glancing blow. Even in God's cursing of mankind there was much grace and mercy. His curses have a boomerang effect.

God's original relationship with mankind was about us serving him and him satisfying us. Adam and Eve sinned and broke that fellowship. Part of the result of that original fall from grace is that now all people seek to be satisfied somewhere other than God. Women tend to seek their ultimate satisfaction in family relationships, often with a husband or child. Men tend to seek their ultimate satisfaction through their work and productivity. But both searches will ultimately be frustrating and never fully satisfying.

Often, a man seeks a sense of significance in his job. He may try for years. He is not fulfilled. In brokenness and desperation, he is driven back to seek his ultimate joy in God alone. His God-given desire for happiness is affected by sin. It leads him to seek happiness in the wrong place and way initially. But when that search for significance fails him, it often drives him back to God in a saving way.

Likewise, many women will seek their deepest sense of security and satisfaction in getting married, having kids, and being the perfect homemaker. This will lead to frustration. It will never be enough. In brokenness and sadness, many women will be driven back to God to find their deepest joy only in him.

God is gracious even in his curses on men and women. Adam probably didn't understand all this that day. But he understood enough. He heard the promise God made about a coming deliverer in Gen 3:15. How do we know? In Gen 3:20 Adam nicknames his wife "mama," (that's essentially what "Eve" means) though they had no kids yet. Why did he do this. He was trusting God's promise that they would not die that day, that they would stay alive, that they would have kids, and that one of their descendants would one day crush Satan's head.

Immediately after this step of faith we are told that God made clothes for Adam and Eve out of animal skins. Adam and Eve had sinned. Their instinct to run, hide, and cover up was right. The problem was their own attempts were futile and ineffective. We can never effectively hide from God. Our only hope is to hide in his provision for us.

Adam and Eve deserved to die that day and suffer God's wrath forever. They did not die. There was a stay of execution. But some innocent animal died that day in their place, so that they could be clothed (Gen 3:21).

"It is impossible for the blood of bulls and goats to take away sins" (Heb 10:4). But throughout the Old Testament animals were used to foreshadow the second Adam, the covenant keeper, "the Lamb of God who takes away the sin of the world" (John 1:29). Adam failed to fulfill his side of the covenant of works. Thus, all humanity was plunged into sin, to live under the curse. Jesus, the second Adam, comes to perfectly fulfill the covenant of works in the place of all his people. He obeyed in all the places we stumble. We all break the law of the covenant. He sinlessly fulfilled the law of the covenant in the place of his people.

At the end of Jesus's life, he should have been crowned and celebrated as King. Yet, he was crucified and condemned under the wrath of God in our stead. Because he lived, died, and rose in our place we can be forgiven. We can be restored into a covenant relationship with God.

God's goodness and generosity is most clearly demonstrated on the cross. Christ willingly left heaven to save us. God the Father punished his own Son in our stead. What more could we ever ask for? He saved us from hell! We should never think of God as stingy or as overly restrictive. He is so lavish and generous it should stagger our imagination!

There are ultimately only two covenants in the Bible whereby mankind can relate to God: the covenant of works and the covenant of grace. God's promise in Gen 3:15 of Christ's coming was the beginning of the covenant of grace. Let us trust such a great God and Savior. Let us, by grace, begin to obey him, though it'll never be perfect obedience in this life. Let us serve him. Let us be satisfied with him in this life and the next. He is such a great God and King!

Chapter 2

Moral Law

What does the word "law" mean when used in the Bible? In the most general sense it means the same thing it does today in modern English. It is a rule, principle, or standard. But it could be used in slightly different ways depending on the context. Sometimes it seems to refer to all of God's written word, as in Ps 1:2. Other times it seems to refer only to the first five books of the Bible, as in Luke 24:44. At times the moral law of God is intended as in Rom 2:14. For the purposes of this book, when we use the word "law," unless otherwise specified, we will be referring to the moral law of God.

What Is the Law?

God's moral law is a revelation of God's heart and character. "God is love" is the shortest summary of God's character found in God's word (1 John 4:8). John Stott says God "is love in his inmost being."[1]

The shortest and best summary of God's law was given by Christ. "'You shall love the Lord your God with all your heart, and with all your soul, and with all your mind.' . . . 'You shall love your neighbor as yourself.' On these two commandments depend the whole Law and the Prophets" (Matt 22:37–40). "Law and the Prophets" was a Jewish way to refer to what we now call the Old Testament. Jesus essentially said, "I'll sum up the whole Bible up until this point for you. Love God and love your neighbor. That is the essence of the moral law."

1. Stott, *Letters of John*, 161.

In a very real sense, the law is just an extension of who God is. The law tells us what God is like and thus what he wants us to be like. Genesis 1:26 says humans were made in God's image. We are to be like him in our character. We are to be loving. We are to love him and all other people.

Think of the Ten Commandments. They are ultimately about love. Don't murder because God loves life and so should you. Don't commit adultery because God loves faithfulness and so should you. Don't lie because God's loves truth and so should you. Don't covet because God loves contentment and so should you. Paul says, "The whole Law is fulfilled in one word . . . 'You shall love your neighbor as yourself'" (Gal 5:14). He teaches the same thing in a more extended fashion in Rom 13:8–10. Love is the way to fulfill the law. Love like God loves. The first four commandments focus on loving God. The last six commandments tell us how to love our neighbor. (In one sense, all the commandments show us how to love God, because God is pleased and honored when we love one another. And all the commandments help us love our neighbor, because the more we love God, we will eventually, inevitably, love our neighbor better.)

Where Is the Law?

What does it mean in Gen 1:26–27 that humans are made in God's image? It means that we have his law and character written on our hearts from the beginning. Westminster Confession of Faith 4.2 states, "He made them . . . and endowed with knowledge, righteousness, and true holiness, in his own image. They had the law of God written in their hearts." "Adam heard as much (of the law) in the garden, as Israel did at Sinai; but only in fewer words, and without thunder."[2]

God is loving, faithful, pure, kind, and so on. So were Adam and Eve when God first made them. Ever since sin entered humanity the image of God has remained in us, though it is cracked. Imagine a full-length mirror in your home. If someone threw a stone and cracked it, you may still be able to see your image in it. But it might be horribly distorted. This is a helpful illustration of how the image of God functions in humanity today. Deep down everyone knows intuitively how to treat other human beings. The clearest evidence is that they know how they want to be treated. Jesus said, "However you want people to treat you, so treat them, for this is the Law and the Prophets" (Matt 7:12). Charlie Munger is known as a rationalist

2. Fisher, *Marrow*, 54.

and a great investor, not a theologian. Yet one of his rules for investment is essentially the golden rule: do unto others what you would have them do unto you.[3] A criminal may have no problem stealing from others. But if someone steals from him, he will be angry. He knows the basics of the law of God in his heart no matter how much he may outwardly deny it. The image of God may be cracked, broken, and nearly erased in the worst of humanity, but the remnant remains in their conscience.

There is no record that God ever said "You shall not murder" in the first four chapters of the Bible. But when Cain killed Abel and God rebuked him, Cain never said "I didn't know that was bad." Deep down he knew it was wrong to murder because it was written on his heart just as it is on my heart and yours.

By Gen 6 humanity became so wicked, God decided to kill almost everyone and start over with Noah. But the implication is that even after all this sin, man was still made and born in God's image (Gen 9:6). Romans 1:19 shows this fact as well. Paul teaches that humans who've never had the Bible are still accountable before God for their sin "because that which is known about God is evident within them; for God made it evident to them." He is speaking, at least in part, of the moral law written on the hearts of even the worst of humanity.

In Rom 2:14–15 he continues his argument. Pagans "who do not have the Law . . . are a law to themselves, in that they show the work of the Law written in their hearts, their conscience bearing witness, and their thoughts alternately accusing or else defending them." Why are cartoons or country songs that refer to an angel on one shoulder whispering good ideas and a devil on the other shoulder whispering evil plans into our minds so universally understood?[4] Because all humans have an inner dialogue going on in our hearts between good and evil. We all know the basics of the law of God, even if it's foggy and fractured in our minds. We also have sin living in us. See Rom 7 for more on that truth. We all have thoughts that sometimes accuse us and other times defend us.

How Is the Law?

Genesis 6:5 says that mankind had become so wicked that "every intent of the thoughts of his heart was only evil continually." Solomon, the wisest

3. Parish, "Munger Operating System," para. 3.
4. See Stapleton, "You Should Probably Leave," as an example.

man before Christ, said that "there is no man who does not sin" (2 Chr 6:36). He also said, "There is not a righteous man on earth who continually does good and who never sins" (Eccl 7:20).

David, one of the godliest men in the Old Testament, said of himself, "I was brought forth in iniquity, And in sin my mother conceived me" (Ps 51:5). He is not saying he was born out of wedlock or any such thing. Rather, he is saying that humans are sinful from the moment of conception. We start off as sinful. We do acts of sin, think thoughts of sin, say words of sin, have feelings of sin, and desire sin because we are already sinful and corrupt. We sin because we are born sinful.

"If we say that we have no sin, we are deceiving ourselves, and the truth is not in us" (1 John 1:8). God's law and the covenant of works were broken, probably on the first day of creation.[5] First Corinthians 15:22 says that "in Adam all die." Romans 5:12 teaches the same truth. Adam was our federal head and representative. When he chose to willfully sin in Gen 3, all humanity was plunged into sin with him whether we like it or not.

We may not like this truth or even accept it. At some level, it doesn't matter. Gravity is real and will affect you whether you say you believe in it or not. And so will man's sinfulness. If you live in a representative democracy such as the United States, you may prize freedom and independence. But we have an elected government that makes decisions for us. So even if you didn't vote for the current president, he is your president if you are a citizen of this country. If you rebel against him and even go as far as to try to kill him, you will likely be caught and prosecuted and convicted and punished. The excuse of "he's not my president" won't hold up in court.

Likewise, at the judgement seat of Christ, the cosmic courtroom of the universe, the argument "I can't be held accountable for my sin because it wasn't really my fault, it was Adam's fault. This isn't fair!" will not hold water either. One of my young sons did something he knew was wrong. When I asked him why, he said, "It's Adam's fault. He chose to eat that apple, Dad."

I laughed at the wisdom of such an answer coming from a child who wasn't even in elementary school yet. I responded, "Buddy, that excuse won't work. Because you chose to sin. And even if you had been made the first man, in Adam's place, in innocence, you would have chosen to sin then as well."

"No way, Dad, not me. I would have never touched that apple, if I had been first in the garden." Again, I laughed.

5. For six reasons why this is true, see Fisher, *Marrow*, 67.

"Buddy, I know you too well. I've been living with you your whole life. And I know you well enough to know you would have chosen to rebel, maybe even quicker than Adam did."

The same could be said of all of us. Look at your own track record. Do we really think we have grounds to protest? We were all conceived dead in our sins. Even if we have been redeemed by Christ, the scars and stains of indwelling sin go deep. We are still marked. We often know clearly the good we should do and in ongoing rebellion choose not to do it.

How is the law of God doing in our day and age? It is broken. It is broken repeatedly. It has been broken more times than we can count since Adam's day until now. But the story is worse than that.

It's not just that God's law is broken, it's also suppressed. When Paul wrote Rom 1, he probably had Gen 3 at least partially in mind. He probably was thinking of pagan people as well that lived far from the influence of the Jewish Scriptures, maybe in faraway places like Spain, where he longed to go and preach. (See Rom 15:20–28 for more on that.)

Romans 1:18–20 teaches that the lost have enough of God's law and revelation in their hearts to be held accountable. But what does unregenerate humanity do with this revelation? They suppress it. They push it down. They resist it. They turn a blind eye. This is a willful blindness more than a blindness of ignorance. They hate the truth and don't want to know the truth. John 3:19–20 says, "Men loved the darkness rather than the light; for their deeds were evil. For everyone who does evil hates light, and does not come to the light, lest his deeds should be exposed."

God doesn't believe in atheists. There's really no such thing. Deep in every human heart is the knowledge of God their creator, even if it is a very shadowy, distant, suppressed, and vague knowledge. It is there. It haunts them and they hate it, and they suppress it willfully, to their own damnation.

There are lots of practical atheists who live as though God didn't exist. They live as if there is no cosmic judge waiting in the next life. Unfortunately, there are many professing Christians who live in a similar way. They play fast and loose with God's law as if it is not real or has little or no bearing on their lives on a day-to-day basis.

Romans 1:21 teaches that all people know there is a God, but they do "not honor Him as God." When we refuse to honor and thank God as we should it leads to a darkening and a deadening. Whatever small glimmer of truth one may have had can be lost through a hardening process as we refuse to honor and praise and thank our Creator. We can "be hardened by the deceitfulness of sin" (Heb 3:13). The more anyone sins, the more our understanding of God can become darker and hazier.

Romans 1:22–32 shows a progression of sin, or maybe we should call it devolution. This darkening leads to arrogance and professed wisdom while we are really ignorant. This leads to idol worship, which often leads to sexual sin and immorality.

We internally exchange God's law for our own opinions on life and morality. We become a law unto ourselves in our own minds. We try to find joy in God's gifts apart from God rather than in worshiping God directly.

This self-centered focus often leads to increasing homosexuality in culture. It eventually leads to a depraved mind. This leads to all kinds of sins listed in verses 29 through 31, including greed and murder and all kinds of sins in between. The whole gamut is seemingly covered.

Paul closes this section in verse 32 by implying three things. All people, even the worst pagan sinners, deep down know there is a God. They further know God has a law we should all obey but don't. They also know we all deserve judgement. There is obviously a remnant of God's law on all people's hearts, whether they will admit it or not.

Application

It is easy to judge others who scandalously break God's law. But a better person to judge at this moment is ourselves. Where do you suppress God's law your own remaining unrighteousness?

Many of us might read Rom 1 as it condemns homosexual sin and shout "Amen" in our hearts. As we see sexual sinfulness dominate so much of our culture, we can gladly rejoice that the Bible speaks so strongly against such deadly sin. But the Bible also takes a very strong stance against greed, gossip, and envy. How are you doing in those areas?

I am not saying there is a moral equivalency to all sins. There is not. All sins are the same primarily in that it only takes any one sin, whether it be lust or murder, to send you to hell. "For whoever keeps the whole law and yet stumbles in one point, he has become guilty of all" (Jas 2:10). But Jesus also said things like "that slave who knew his master's will and did not get ready or act in accord with his will shall receive many lashes, but the one who did not know it, and committed deeds worthy of a flogging, will receive but few" (Luke 12:47–48). The point is clear. Sins done in ignorance are still punished, but not as badly as willful sins. Some sins are worse than others. Likewise, "Woe to you, Bethsaida! For if the miracles had been performed in Tyre and Sidon which occurred in you, they would have repented long ago, sitting in sackcloth and ashes. But it will be more tolerable for Tyre and Sidon in the judgement, than for you" (Luke 10:13–14). We will be judged to some degree based on the insight, light, and revelation we have. The argument could be made that a murderer in northern Africa who never heard any biblical truth may be judged more lightly in hell than an greedy American who ignored biblical truth from his family, church, and radio every week.

The Westminster Shorter Catechism question and answer 83 says, "Are all transgression of the law equally sinful? Some sins, because of their nature and the circumstances, are more sinful in the sight of God than others." It is better to get sinfully angry at your neighbor in your heart and call them a fool behind their back than to shoot them in the head with a gun. But if you don't repent of your sinful anger, you will still go to hell.

Here's my point. Read slowly through the list from Rom 1:29–31 and see if you notice any discernible pattern: "Being filled with all unrighteousness, wickedness, greed, evil; full of envy, murder, strife, deceit, malice; they are gossips, slanderers, haters of God, insolent, arrogant, boastful, inventors of evil, disobedient to parents, without understanding, untrustworthy, unloving, unmerciful." It seems that Paul is jumbling up many big sins with lots of little sins. "Envy, murder, strife, deceit." We might be quick to say "yes I envy and I have lied, but I've never murdered and I'm very peaceable and try to avoid strife." The point is everyone is convicted by this list if you're paying attention.

I wonder how the growing church in Rome first heard these words of Paul when read to them. Maybe they cheered and amened as Paul condemned many of the wicked, outward, obvious sins of the pagans surrounding them in Rome in the first century. I wonder if they grew more quiet, solemn, and humble as this list was read.

Where do you personally suppress the truth in your own life? Maybe you are slightly convinced that you drink too much alcohol on a regular basis. You know Eph 5:18 says that drunkenness is a sin. But how exactly do you define drunkenness anyway? Is having a buzz being drunk? One beer, two beers, three beers, ten; who knows how many are too many? The conviction may come from time to time on Friday night, but it's easy to push down because at least you're not sinning as much as those wicked politicians in Washington, DC.

"Yes, I gossip a little, but technically all I say is true! At least I'm not a liar and a cheat like my friend." We remain experts at blame-shifting and minimizing, just like our first parents in the garden. We exchange God's clear moral law for our personal interpretation, which we tend to water down when it gets too close to home. Our sinful desire is still to be our own God and set our own laws for life.

Conclusion

We were all born into the covenant of works as sinners and failures, fully deserving God's just wrath from day one. We all willingly chose to sin and break God's law. God the Father made Jesus, who never committed any sin, "to be sin on our behalf, that we might become the righteousness of God in [Christ]" (2 Cor 5:21). What glorious news. God sent his one and only Son to become man and live as a substitute in the place of all the people who would ever trust in Christ. He never broke the law but always sinlessly kept it.

We exchange the truth of God for a lie. God exchanged his righteous Son for his sinful people. Jesus was put in our place, on the cross, under the wrath of God for sin. He never broke the law. But on the cross God treated him like the ultimate lawbreaker.

When we look to the life, death, and resurrection of Christ in our place by faith we are saved. We are forgiven. We can now stand blameless before God's judgement. Wrath fell on Christ for us. We are free. Our sinful record has been exchanged by grace for his righteous record, credited to our accounts. Christ suffered hell on the cross for his people so that we can go to heaven.

Chapter 3

Covenant of Grace

In Gen 3 when God did not instantly kill Adam and Eve for their sin and lawbreaking, the covenant of grace was introduced. A shadowy promise was made to Adam and Eve in God's curse on Satan. They would live. They would have babies. One of their descendants would be bruised by Satan but would crush his head. Later, God killed some animal to provide clothes to cover Adam and Eve's sinful shame. This foreshadowed the coming of the Lord Jesus to live and die in his people's place so that we can be clothed in his righteous record like a royal, spotless robe. His law-keeping and covenant-keeping can become ours by faith.

Genesis 4–11 covers centuries of human history, but there aren't many high notes. There is a lot of sin, lawbreaking, death, and destruction. People are murdered; God's standards are broken. God sends a flood to wipe out most of humanity. God separates people at the tower of Babel as further punishment for sin. There were not many heroes during those years. Genesis 6:5 is a good summary of those times: "Then the LORD saw that the wickedness of man was great on the earth, and that every intent of the thoughts of his heart was only evil continually." Things seemingly went from bad to worse. In Gen 12 God starts to work with one man named Abram.

In this chapter we will look at God's covenant with Abraham. It is helpful to know from the start that it is an extension of the covenant of grace that started in Gen 3. What God had started in the garden in a shadowy way he now begins to make more clear and obvious in this Abrahamic expression of grace.

Fear

Genesis 11–12 tells us that when Abram was seventy-five years old his wife Sarai was barren, and they had no children. His family was wealthy. God spoke to him and told him to leave his extended family and his current living situation and go to a new land. God did not say exactly where. He did not give many details at all. He essentially said, "Trust me. Pack up and start moving."

God told Abe that he would give him a huge family, a family so big and important it would become a nation unto itself. And this nation would become so special and important that it would bless all the other families on planet earth. God told him that he would have the protection of God on his life. "I will bless those who bless you, And the one who curses you I will curse" (Gen 12:3). Abram trusts God and so he obeys. True trust always leads to obedience.

In Gen 15 we find Abram in a place of fear. It's been twenty-five years since God first spoke to Abram and there doesn't seem to be much progress. Abram obeyed but had little to show for it. He certainly didn't have a huge family; no nation had come from his loins. He still didn't have any children at all. He seems to be in a place of fear, doubt, and frustration. God speaks and tells him not to be afraid. But realistically, it seems that the circumstances were shouting to him that he should be afraid. He was one hundred years old with no descendants. That was often seen as a curse in those days. He had much wealth he had accumulated but no one to give it to. If he died at this point, one of his servants would benefit because there was no one to carry on his name and lineage. Have you ever been in such a spot where it seems like the deck is stacked against you? Have you ever trusted God and obeyed and expected good things in return and come up empty-handed? Have you ever "waited on the Lord" and felt like your patience and perseverance were in vain? If so, you might be in good company.

Abe prayed to God, saying in essence, "You've made me these big promises, God. And yes, you've protected me as you said you would. You've blessed me with many possessions. But what good is all this if I have no kids and I die and have no one to leave it to? I thought I was going to have a big family. That's what I deeply want. I don't want to leave all my possessions to a mere servant, but to a son!"

If God always gave us his rewards instantly we would have little to no faith. We wouldn't need it. But delays are the problem. In the waiting we struggle.

Hebrews 11:6 teaches that God rewards those that seek him, and believing that is an integral part of true saving faith. Believing that God exists and is real is pretty easy and obvious based on the complexity of creation and our conscience. Believing that God is good is another matter altogether. Read biblical accounts of Satan's attacks and temptations against Adam, Eve, Job, Jesus. Satan never seems to try to convince them that God was not real. He does always, in different ways, try to convince them, and us, that God is not good and trustworthy.

We doubt God will protect us. We doubt he will provide for us. We doubt he will promote our interests in the best way and in the best time. In our doubts and fears we begin to assume that we must do it ourselves. I must look out for number one!

But this leads to gnawing insecurity. Deep down we know we can't fully protect ourselves. There's no guarantee we can provide for ourselves sufficiently. Sometimes it's awkward to be promoting ourselves all the time. We are weak, frail, fragile, and fickle. This reality leads us to be overwhelmed by fear.

One commentator says, "Faith is a problem . . . when it clings to the problematic present. . . . In our impatience we are prone to conclude that if it is not given now, it will not be given."[1] Do you see this in your own life? If God has made a clear promise to you in his word, but you are not experiencing any of the realities of that promise, do you tend to doubt that you ever will? We can get so focused on our present suffering that we miss the glory and hope of the future God has guaranteed for us.

Joyce Baldwin says, "God's delays are not denials."[2] But we often think they are. Maybe we've been praying for something for twenty years, such as the salvation of a child. We can begin to despair that it will ever happen. God's best plan may be to save that child at age twenty-three. Our job is to hold fast to biblical promises and pray in faith and hope and not give in to doubt and despair.

I've taught four different fifteen-year-olds how to drive. Another way to describe that is sitting in the passenger seat, being out of control, and worrying the whole time! But if a seasoned, mature driver that you trust is driving, you should be able to relax and even take a nap if you can get comfortable in the passenger seat. If you truly trust God to rule and reign and guide your life well, relax! I'm not saying you need to sleep through your

1. Brueggemann, *Genesis*, 147–49.

2. Baldwin, *Genesis 12–50*, 51.

whole life. But there ought to be a sense of inner peace amidst the outward turmoil of life if I truly believe God rules all things for my good. Jesus in his humanity had no problem sleeping in a small boat in the middle of a terrible storm. How did he do it? He fully trusted the perfect plan of his Father.

If you see a duck swimming across a pond, the duck's body seems to be motionless on top of the water. The duck seems to be still yet gliding quickly across the surface of the water. The duck seems propelled by some magical force or wind. But below the surface, its little webbed feet are paddling as hard as they can to generate the force to move.

Christians should be like an upside-down duck. Here's what I mean. Someone who has strong faith in God ought to work hard in life. They ought to be faithful to do all the duties that God has put in front of them. They go to work, they pray, they love their spouse, they raise their kids, they pay their bills, they share their faith with their neighbors, they give money away, they serve the poor, etc. But inwardly a Christian should be at total rest. Outwardly, they may be moving fast and sweating and exerting energy. That is right and good. Inwardly, they should be in a state of peace and tranquility. There ought to be a mental and spiritual attitude that says, "I work hard as unto the Lord. I parent hard as unto the Lord. But I cannot guarantee good results from my work or parenting etc. Only the Lord can do that. So, I do my part. But I don't trust my part. I trust the Lord to bless the work of my hands in the best time and proper way and give the results he deems best. I trust him and rest." "Unless the Lord builds the house, / They labor in vain who build it" (Ps 127:1). The Psalm doesn't tell the workman to put down his tools and nap while God miraculously builds a house. Rather, keep doing your work as best you can, but don't trust in your efforts to prevail. Trust in God's goodness to give the best results in due time. Easier said than done.

Faith

In Gen 15:4 God speaks and tells Abe that he will give him a son. God promises to keep his word. God then tells him to go outside and try to count the stars. Maybe at best Abe could have counted four thousand with his naked eye if he had tried. But even with the best telescopes you cannot see and count them all. God tells him that is a picture of how many descendants he will have.

God is going to do something so big through Abe his little finite mind cannot even conceive or handle all the implications. His mental circuits would be blown if God showed him all he would do.

God seems to imply as well, "I made all those stars in a day. It was easy. I'll give you as many kids as I want when I want without one ounce of trouble. Trust me!"

God gave him no evidence or proof. He only gave his words. He gave reassurance. And Abe believed him. Abe trusted. Abe rested on God's good word.

Romans 10:17 teaches that faith starts and grows by hearing, listening to, paying attention to, trusting, and believing God's good word. Genesis 15:6 is a crucial verse: "Then he believed in the Lord; and He reckoned it to him as righteousness." It is quoted multiple times in the New Testament.

How were people saved in the Old Testament? Essentially just like we are in New Testament times. Romans 4, especially verses 3 through 8, make this very clear. We look back towards a risen Messiah by grace alone through faith alone. They looked forward to a shadowy Messiah by grace alone through faith alone.

We see much more than they did. But they saw enough. They trusted in the promised child of Gen 3:15, the promised offspring, the promised heir to come, the snake crusher, the Messiah, the Christ.

Abe trusted God. He rested on his promise. He put his faith in God's plan, provision, protection, and timing. He did not trust in his own plan and provision.

Did that make Abe sinlessly perfect? No. Wait until Gen 16 when he starts sleeping with the maid. But legally, in the cosmic courtroom of the universe, God said, "If you trust me, I'll treat you like you are blameless, like you are just, like you are fully right with me." Abe trusted. And God treated him as righteous by faith!

Imagine if you had $100,000 in your bank account but, through many foolish and sinful decisions, that had somehow become $30,000 in deficit. You are desperate to fix your financial situation but unable to. You go to the bank and beg for mercy. They forgive the debt. They cancel it and set your account back to $0. That's wonderful! But it's not necessarily the best thing. Because you still have no money, and if one more check or expense hits your account, you are right back in the hole.

But what if the bank felt extra generous that day and said, "We'll cover your deficit and go ahead and give you another $100,000 to get you back to financial strength!" That's better than mere pardon or forgiveness. In spiritual terms, that's called justification. And that's what God did for Abe that day. He did not just wipe out his sin debt and get him to zero. He counted him as truly righteous in his sight. That's what he does today for all who truly trust in Christ.

God goes on to tell Abe that he would keep his promise to give him the land that he had promised him as well. Abe responds by asking God how he could know for sure. When your faith is weak and struggling, it is not wrong to ask God for assurances if you do it in a humble and needy way rather than an arrogant and demanding way.

I'll be honest. This does not seem like very strong faith to me. It seems like a bare minimum, struggling faith. And yet, it is true faith and thus it saves.

The most important thing about our faith is not the quality of our faith but the object of our faith. It is better to have weak faith in a strong Savior than to have strong faith in a false savior. Cling to Christ as tightly as you can by faith. But don't trust in the strength of your faith. Trust in the strength of your Savior.

Romans 4:18 says, "In hope against hope he believed." God's promises were seemingly impossible, yet Abe held on by faith. "And without becoming weak in faith he contemplated his own body, now as good as dead since he was about a hundred years old" (Rom 4:19). This probably means that Abe knew he was old and impotent. Practically speaking he was totally unable to do his part to produce a kid. This is not blind faith. He is thinking practically about the problem. But he is letting God's promise trump his own present circumstances, feelings, and experiences.

But he did not give up or give in to doubt. As he meditated on God's word, his faith grew even in the face of seemingly impossible promises (Rom 4:20–21). Maybe Abe preached truth to himself in his mind like this: "I can't produce a child. But God can. I know he can do whatever he wants!"

The Bible is so realistic. Even the so-called heroes of the faith are presented to us honestly, warts and all, doubts and all, struggles and all. God shows us their flaws and failures so we can relate and have hope that we are in good company when we waver and falter.

Abe's faith was not easy, laid-back faith. It was an active, wrestling, grappling faith. It reminds me of the father of the demon-possessed boy who said to Jesus, "I do believe; help my unbelief" (Mark 9:24). Jesus answered that man's prayer immediately with great power. He did not demand that the man have perfect faith, only sincere and honest faith.

Jesus prefers we have a humble faith that struggles rather than a so-called faith filled with hubris and presumption. Be honest with God in prayer about your doubts and fears. But humbly submit them to his words and then take the risky steps of faith or the steps of patience he calls you to.

Maybe your prayers at time will sound like this: "God, I am trying my best to believe. Help me. How can I know for sure what you will do, when you will do it, and even if you will do it? This is hard; I'm struggling. But I want to trust you. Please help me rest in your word." I believe God loves to answer such honest and humble prayers.

Wrestle in prayer when your faith is weak and struggling. God is so gracious. He condescends to accept baby faith, weak faith, struggling faith, mustard-seed-size faith. Do you wrestle regularly, honestly in prayer like this with the Lord? You should.

If you are angry with God or doubting God, tell him. He already knows. Throw off your self-righteous attempts to pretend that doubt isn't in your heart. Do not try to fake it before you make it with God. Do not try and pretend to be better than you are. Be as real and raw with him as you can.

Look how God responds to Abe in Gen 15. Look at how God responds to the man in Mark 9. This is his pattern with the lowly. There is a proud, scoffing way to question God, like Zacharias did when the angel told him he would have John the Baptist as a child late in life. The angel rebuked him and made him unable to speak for nine months. But, even then, he still had a child! Even in that, God shows great mercy, grace, generosity, and love! See Luke 1:17–20 for more on this story.

There is a humble, curious, confused, and weak way to ask God "How will this happen? How can I know?"—like the virgin Mary and Abe did (Luke 1:32–35). God honors the honesty and humility of such prayers. He may not give all the answers we want. But such a struggling faith honors him.

Fulfillment

In Gen 12:9–12 God essentially says, "Abe, you want a sign to help faith? Go get some animals and cut them in half." Abe does what God says and then a terror starts to come over him because he knows what this means. He knows what God is doing.

In the ancient near east, when you wanted to make a treaty, you didn't get out pen and paper and call the lawyers to draw up a legal contract to sign. Rather there was a ritual ceremony that was performed. Often some powerful king of a large nation might come to a small nearby city-state. The king of the large nation would say to the leader of this potential vassal state, "I will protect you from all the other terrible warring tribes and nations in this region. But you must swear loyalty to me and pay me some tribute or taxes." If the city-state agreed, animals would be cut in half and laid out so there was in essence an aisle between the separate parts. The leader of the city-state would walk through the separate pieces, declaring the terms of the covenant of loyalty he was making with the great king. Sometimes the king might walk through the pieces, declaring his side of the bargain. Often, he would not. He had all the power and so did not have to prove his loyalty to a weaker subordinate.

As the weaker party in the covenant walked through the slain pieces of animals the message was clear. If I break loyalty to you, I will be slaughtered and cut in half as these pieces have been. God is using this ancient treaty-making ceremony to make a covenant with Abram.

Abe trembles because he realizes he will never be able to perfectly keep his end of the bargain. He won't be able to always fully trust in God. He's already struggling as it is.

To make a treaty with a mighty king such as the Pharaoh of Egypt would be bad enough. But to make a treaty obligation with the King of the whole universe, who knows and sees all, is terrifying and maddening. Abe even then was flooded with fear, doubt, and worry.

Genesis 15:13–16 is a prophecy of Israel's four hundred years of slavery in Egypt. It seems like a strange place to give such a dark prophecy. But the sense seems to be that God is saying, "Abram, it will often be this way between me and my people. I will make them great promises, such as a promised land flowing with milk and honey and abundance. But they won't experience it immediately. They will have to wait many generations to experience it. My people must live by faith. I am good, trustworthy, and always keep my promises, but my people must learn to wait. You must learn to wait. You must learn to trust me fully even when everything looks bleak."

Then, "there appeared a smoking oven and a flaming torch which passed between these pieces" (Gen 15:17). What in the world is this, and what does this signify? God appeared as fire and smoke as he would later at Mount Sinai (Exod 19:18). God was the great King of the universe. Abe was the little leader of a tiny family. God was making covenant with Abe. But God was not forcing Abe to walk through the pieces and declare the stipulations of the covenant. God was doing that. God was taking Abe's place.

In some sense, God took the responsibility for Abram's part. God walked through the pieces. God made covenant with Abe. God swore to give the promised land to Abe's descendants. God was saying through his actions, "Abram, if you or your descendants break covenant, I will be slaughtered in your place. I will be torn to pieces for the sake of the covenant."

A covenant here could be defined as a "unilateral treaty made in blood with implications." It is unilateral because it is made by one party. There was no negotiation. God just made the covenant with Abe. It is made in blood because death is the consequence of breaking it. It has massive implications for how Abram should live as a result.

Sometimes people speak of conditional or unconditional covenants. But that is not the most helpful language in this case. What's important to note is that this was not a negotiation between two peers hammering out a deal. God just made the deal. In this way, it feels very unconditional. Yet there are massive implications.[3] Of course in response Abe was expected to trust and obey God.

In this sense the covenant of grace is very much like an adoption in modern times. Parents go to an orphanage. They see a young child, maybe even an infant, they want to adopt. The child has no say whatsoever in the matter. The parents choose the child and bring the child home, probably after paying tens of thousands of dollars. The child had no say in the matter. In that sense it was unconditional; unilateral. But as the child grows up in this adoptive family, there will be massive implications flowing from the covenant. The adopted child will be expected to honor, trust, and obey the parents, even as the parents continue to sacrifice, love, and provide for the child.

God has spoken to Abe multiple times about the land that he has promised to give to his people. But now he speaks in a perfect verb, a verb of completion, as though it's already done and a present reality. "To your descendants I have given this land" (Gen 15:18). When God speaks, it is as good as done, even if the fulfillment is four hundred years away.

3. Ferguson, *Whole Christ*, 116.

God doesn't say, "I will give this land." He says, "I have given this land to your descendants" who don't even exist yet. Abe still has no kids! Not even one! Yet God speaks of a whole nation of descendants and expects Abe to trust him by faith!

When God speaks it is a done deal. You can take it to the bank. Better, you can bank your whole life on it. You may not see fulfillment with your physical eyes yet. But you can see it with the eyes of faith.

Application

Where in life are you currently struggling with fear? All fear other than fearing God is sin. All sin is rooted in doubt (Rom 14:23). Where are you doubting God will reward you?

How's your prayer life? Do you wrestle in prayer honestly with God like Abram did? Can you vent your frustrations to him humbly? This is a practical key to getting through such trying times. Often God will put us in trying situations to see if we obey him only for temporal rewards we can experience now. He wants us to obey even if the rewards may only come and be experienced in the next life.

It would be easy at this point for any of us to say, "Abram got a personal visitation from God. He got a voice from on high. He saw a vision. He got personal experience and personal covenant ceremony! Of course he had faith in hard times. I've had none of that!"

We can be tempted to think if we lived in the Old Testament times it might have been better. Maybe we could have had an exciting, confirming experience like Abram and others. I have often felt that way.

Conclusion

There is a better experience to be had in these New Testament days we live in. "The new covenant era brings richer fellowship with God, greater liberty, and a fuller outpouring of the Holy Spirit."[4] There's also a better example of wrestling in prayer when you're tempted to doubt. Abram proved to be a great man of faith and prayer. But there's still one greater.

If any man ever had reason to fear and doubt that God was good and that God would keep his promise, it was the Lord Jesus Christ as he hung on the cross. As he hung, suspended between heaven and earth, stripped

4. Crowe, *Path of Faith*, 93.

naked, wearing our sin and shame, he suffered. The greatest suffering was not physical. The greatest pain he felt that day was being forsaken by his God. His Father's smile was not felt by Christ, and hell was dumped on him for the sins of all his people.

What did Jesus do in that moment? He prayed. He wrestled honestly with his Father about the doubt he was tempted to feel. "My God, My God, why hast Thou forsaken me?" (Matt 27:46). In that moment he did not call God his Father as he typically did. He wasn't experiencing God as Father but as Judge.

Essentially, he prayed, "I don't like this. I don't want this. How long will this last? It doesn't feel like I can take it any longer!" But God did give him peace. He died well in faith: "Father, into Thy hands I commit my spirit" (Luke 23:46).

We were not there to see this moment of the covenant of grace. Neither were the Galatians who made up the church Paul wrote to, decades later. Yet, Gal 3:1 says, "You foolish Galatians, who has bewitched you, before whose eyes Jesus Christ was publicly portrayed as crucified?"

When someone hears or reads the message of Christ crucified for them with ears or eyes of faith, it is as good as if they were there watching Christ die for them. We have not seen a flaming firepot and smoking oven flying through split carcasses. But if we have trusted in Christ for salvation, we have seen a greater miracle than that.

God became man. He lived the perfect life we are meant to live under the covenant of works. He got to the end of his life and should have been crowned and celebrated as King of the universe. Yet, he was condemned, crucified, and killed as the worst criminal in the universe. This was the fulfillment of the covenant of grace. This was what the original ceremony pointed to. God walked through the split pieces in our place, saying that if we sinned, he would not rip us apart but would rather rip himself apart. Christ on the cross was ripped apart by God's wrath in our place.

Christ is the true seed of Abram. He is the true covenant keeper. We are the covenant breakers. He took the curse you and I justly deserve. This is the basis for our only true hope.

In this life we will go through dark, hard, tempting, and trying times. They are tests ordained by God. Will we trust him fully when we are getting no earthly rewards?

Look at the cross. Look to the risen Savior. He is our joy. He is our confidence. He is our peace. Do not fear. Christ is our shield from God's wrath. Christ is our eternal reward!

Chapter 4

Mosaic Covenant

Before you read this chapter, I have a brief exercise for you. Quickly write down your answer to this question. If you had an opportunity on a short elevator ride to share the gospel with someone, how would you do it? Assume the person you're talking to has grown up in America so has at least heard of Christ and the Bible. Perhaps they see a Bible in your hand on the elevator and say to you, "You know, I've been wondering lately, what does a person have to do to be saved? I'm interested in becoming a Christian and being right with God? How can I do that?" If you were asked the question, how would you answer? At least think about that for a moment before you read on.

Ultimately, we are looking at how Christians are supposed to relate to the moral law of God in their lives. This can seem like a simple question, but it has aspects that make it complicated. For that reason, we started at the very beginning. God made a covenant with Adam, sometimes called the covenant of life, or of creation, or of works. The covenant of works is probably the most common name. The Westminster Confession of Faith 7.2 and 19.1, and Shorter Catechism answer 12, speak to this reality.

Adam was our representative, our federal head. When he fell into sin, all humanity, including you and I, fell with him. (See Rom 5:12 for more on this.) Adam broke God's moral law and the covenant of works in Gen 3. Yet God in grace and mercy came pursuing Adam immediately after. God could have come in wrath, but he didn't. In Gen 3:15 God made a promise that Adam and Eve would stay alive and have babies. One day, many generations later, another human would come, a second Adam of sorts, the head of a new spiritual race of humanity. He would do battle with the serpent as well. He would be wounded by Satan. Where Adam had sinned and failed, this snake crusher would fight, win, and prevail in our place. This promise ushered in the beginning of the covenant of grace.

When it comes to relating to God there are only two ways. You can relate to God through the first Adam and the covenant of works or you can relate to God through the second Adam and the covenant of grace. There is no third way, no other option. You see both the covenant of grace and the covenant of works side by side in Gen 3. The covenant of works brought curses on humanity because of their sin. Justice was executed, at least partially. (Adam and Eve were kicked out of the garden for their sin.) But mercy was also extended in the covenant of grace because Adam and Eve didn't die physically that day. They were not cut off and condemned to hell as they deserved. Thus, in one chapter, the covenant of works and the covenant of grace stood side by side with their corresponding results.

Later in Genesis we see God drawing near in grace to another man, Abram (later called Abraham) in Gen 12, 15, and 17. The covenant of grace is expanded and explained more clearly than it was in the garden. God is seeking to bring more clarity to this great covenant with men.

In this chapter we will look at the Mosaic covenant. One question we must address is: Is the Mosaic covenant an extension of the covenant of works or of the covenant of grace? What do you think? Some Christians disagree about the answer.

My best understanding, after much study, is that the Mosaic covenant is an extension of both covenants. This may seem crazy at first, but let me try to explain. In Gen 3 we see both covenants side by side, and that's not the only place.

Think about this. Did Jesus come to talk about the covenant of works or the covenant of grace? The answer is both as well!

Do you remember the famous story where Jesus interacts with a man we often refer to as the rich young ruler? This story is told in Matt 19, Mark 10, and Luke 18. I'll give a brief rehearsal from the "Olan translation." (This is not a real translation!)

A man runs up to Jesus and says, "What must I do to inherit eternal life?" Now think about that for a minute. When's the last time that happened to you? I wish that happened to me daily, but it rarely does. It's such a soft ball. It presents such an easy opportunity to be bold for Jesus! But Jesus's own answer may surprise us.

Jesus responds, "Well, you know the Ten Commandments; just keep those and you'll be fine." Have you ever responded this way to a salvation question? What in the world is our Savior doing?

The man clarifies, "Which commandments?" This is a big deal. Salvation is on the line; he needs to be sure he obeys the right ones. Jesus basically summarizes the second half of the Ten Commandments.

Why did Jesus do this? Maybe he didn't understand the question. I don't want to spend the whole chapter diagnosing this great passage. But the bottom line is Jesus was speaking out of the covenant of works to this man. This wasn't the only time Jesus had an interaction like this. See Luke 10:25–29 for another example.

There are places in the Bible that, taken out of context, can make it seem as though God's plan for salvation is the covenant of works. Many so-called Christian denominations fall into this trap. We must be careful to avoid it while also taking the words of Christ seriously and understanding them accurately.

Technically there are two ways to be right with God. If someone could come into the world innocent like Adam and Eve did and keep the moral law perfectly for as long as God wanted them to, they would remain right with God. They would not need a salvation experience. They would not need Christ as their substitute. But this way has been ruined for us all because we are all now born dead in our sins because of the sin of Adam.

Sometimes in our self-righteousness and pride we need to be reminded of our sin. The covenant of works is a great way to do that. That is at least in part what Jesus was doing with the rich young ruler. Someone once told me that in evangelism we should give law to the proud and grace to the humble.[1] It seems that Christ was giving law to a proud man that day.

But for our purposes it's important to see that the covenant of works is still in function on planet earth and that it has a role in helping us better understand how the covenant of grace works and how much we should value the covenant of grace. But it can become confusing at times. The church at Galatia in the first century struggled with such confusion. Let's look at how Paul explained this.

1. My friend Kent Bailey told me this and was not sure of the original source..

Covenant of Works

It will be helpful to remember something crucial in this chapter and for the rest of the book. Paul had many great spiritual concepts in his mind, more than you and I do for sure. But he did not have all the same language and semantics that you and I do. We have had the privilege of almost two thousand years of theological study and development that Paul didn't have. I'm not saying a theologian today is smarter or godlier than Paul. I am saying we may have the benefit of some helpful terminology and shorthand phrases that had not been invented yet.

The clearest example of this may be the word "Trinity." It is not found in the Bible. The concept is certainly there, but not the word. The shorthand for our Triune God,"Trinity," had not been developed yet. Paul knew the reality of Trinity better than you and I. But we have language to talk about the Triune God in a simpler and clearer way.

Likewise, Paul won't be using the terminology "covenant of grace" or "covenant of works," but the concepts are certainly in his mind. Rather than talk about those under the covenant of works, Paul might say "as many as are of the works of the Law" (Gal 3:10) and mean "as many as are of the covenant of works." Keep this in mind as we move ahead into some hard territory.

In Gal 3:10 Paul says, "For as many as are of the works of the Law are under a curse." What does he mean by this? Paul uses this phrase to talk about anyone who is relating to God via the covenant of works. They are depending on their own law-keeping, their doing of good works as described by God's law, to make them right with God. But God says that always ends in being cursed because we must be perfect to be right with God because he is perfect. "Cursed is everyone who does not abide by all things written in the book of the law, to perform them" (Gal 3:10). So, if you seek to be right with God by obeying God then you must obey everything written down in the Old Testament to achieve your goal. It is impossible for us.

We all come into life under the covenant of works because of the sin of Adam. Hebrews 7:9–10 is making an argument that the priesthood of Melchizedek is greater than the priesthood of Levi because when Abraham paid tithes to Melchizedek, Levi "was still in the loins of" Abraham (Heb 7:10). Levi was a descendant of Abraham. Abraham paid tithes to Melchizedek, which shows Mel is greater than Abraham. But because Levi descended from Abraham, Abraham represented Levi. So, if Mel was greater than Abraham, Levi's representative, then Mel is obviously greater than Levi as well. The same argument can be applied to you and me and Adam. Adam was our representative. He died in his sins. He broke the covenant of works. We were in his loins when he sinned. So now all of Adam's descendants come to planet earth already dead in our sins, having broken the covenant of works in and through our representative.

Paul essentially repeats the same truth in Gal 3:11. No one can be justified by obeying the law. He quotes Hab 2:4 as proof that this was always true, even in the Old Testament: "The righteous man shall live by faith." In Old and New Testament times people are justified before God by faith, not by law-keeping. Westminster Confession of Faith 11.6 says, "The justification of believers under the Old Testament was in all these respects identical with the justification of believers under the New Testament."

Galatians 3:12 reiterates the same point. If you seek to be saved by law-keeping, then you are not seeking to be saved by faith. The two different ways of salvation, the different covenants, are antithetical to one another. He quotes Lev 18:5 this time to make his point that it has always been this way, even in the time of Moses. The two different ways of salvation are like oil and water. They do not mix at all!

So many false teachers, whether intentionally or unintentionally, in our day and in the days of Paul, seek to confuse the two covenants. Most of them may never use the word "covenant," but that is still what they are doing when they try to add law-keeping as a prerequisite of salvation by faith. I've never met anyone who teaches salvation by pure law-keeping. But I've met many who teach salvation by faith plus works. I heard a Mormon once say, "It's like if your parents were going to buy you a $100 bike but they wanted you to contribute a little, maybe only a quarter. Salvation is mostly by faith in God, but there are some works we must contribute." If you add any law-keeping to salvation by faith as a means to be saved, you have ruined the concept of salvation by grace alone, through faith alone, in Christ alone. (Mormons also are wrong about the deity of Christ and other issues as well. I'm just using this as an example of a salvation-by-faith-plus-works system.)

All people are born into this world under the covenant of works (because of Adam's original sin) and therefore under a curse. We all deserve to die for our sin. We all will die eternally for our sin, unless someone else dies for us and takes the curse for us.

Covenant of Grace

When Christ died on the cross under the wrath of God, he was taking the curse for sin that you and I deserve because of our law breaking. Paul quotes Deut 21:23, saying, "Cursed is everyone who hangs on a tree" (Gal 3:13). We deserved to be hung on that tree, yet he was. Christ was fulfilling the punishment that we deserved for our having broken the covenant of works. In doing so, he set free from the covenant of works anyone who would trust in him as their substitute.

God made the covenant of grace very clear to Abraham and his family as we saw in the last chapter. But by the work of Jesus, any gentile, any non-Jew, can become a recipient of the covenant of grace. You don't have to be a physical descendant of Abraham to be a spiritual descendant of Abraham by faith.

If two humans make a covenant, such as marriage, you cannot just set it aside later as though it did not matter or as if it had no significance or lasting value. Nor can you arbitrarily add extra conditions to it later. Imagine a man and woman are married. Five years later the man decides he wants to add a prenup. The woman would have to agree to this addition. He could not just add that stipulation back into a covenant that had already been ratified and in effect.

Paul makes a very similar argument in Gal 3:15–17. God made the covenant of grace abundantly clear to Abraham for Abraham and his family (which would become the nation of Israel.) Over four hundred years later, God made the Mosaic covenant, which Paul refers to simply as "the Law" (Gal 3:17). God made a radically free promise to Abraham in Genesis. What God did later in Exodus with Abraham's descendants was in no way meant to diminish the glory and freedom of that promise. Rather, it was meant to highlight the graciousness of that promise. Thomas Boston, a great Puritan writer, teaches that "there is no confounding of the two covenants of grace and works; but the latter was added to the former as subservient unto it, to turn their eyes towards the promise, or covenant of grace."[2] God used the Mosaic covenant to remind the nation of Israel of their sin but also of the covenant of grace they had in Abraham.

God had made the covenant of grace with Adam in Gen 3. In Gen 12–17 God made the covenant of grace clearer and more explicit. If anything, he deepened the promises of the covenant of grace. It got better and clearer, not worse. And this is exactly what God did with Moses in Exodus.

2. Quoted in Fisher, *Marrow*, 77.

The covenant of grace was supposed to get better, clearer, and deeper, not worse by any stretch of the imagination.

Paul makes the point that if God wanted the promised inheritance to come to Abraham's people by law-keeping then it could no longer be based on promise alone. But God had already given his word that the inheritance would come to Abraham's people "by means of a promise" (Gal 3:18). Then why, when we read Exodus through Deuteronomy, which contains the Mosaic covenant, does there seem to be so much law in these four books?

God was again setting the covenant of works and the covenant of grace side by side as he had done in Gen 3. In Rom 10:5 Paul teaches that Moses did write about the covenant of works: "Moses writes that the man who practices the righteousness which is based on law shall live by that righteousness." If you can perfectly practice the law, then you will be right with God based on your perfect law-keeping. Leviticus 18:5 and Deut 27:26 are two verses where this is clear.

But Paul goes on in Rom 10:6–8 to quote from Deut 30:10–15, also written by Moses. When Paul quotes these verses, he says that this is not righteousness based on law, but righteousness based on faith. In the Mosaic covenant, specifically in Deut 27–30, the righteousness by law and the righteousness by faith are set side by side. The covenant of works and the covenant of grace are set side by side in the Mosaic covenant.

Why the Mosaic Covenant

Often when I study Rom 10 or Gal 3, I sometimes literally find myself saying out loud, "God, why did you do it this way? Why did you make it so confusing?!" Often, I feel frustrated or exasperated and confused. I wonder if any of you can identify with me just having read the last couple of pages.

I think Paul at times must have felt the same way, or at least he anticipated that some of his readers would think that way. In Gal 3:19 Paul asks, "Why the Law then?" By "Law" he means the Mosaic covenant. Why did God add the Mosaic covenant? Wouldn't it have been much easier to make the covenant with Abraham by grace alone, through faith alone, by promise, not by works, and then just skip straight ahead to Jesus as the fulfillment? Leave out all this confusing Mosaic law stuff. It just seems to muddy the waters of salvation!

The Mosaic law, the Mosaic covenant, "was added because of transgressions" (Gal 3:19). What in the world does that mean? Paul clarifies again in Gal 3:21 that the Mosaic law is in no way "contrary to the promise of God[.] May it never be! For if a law had been given which was able to impart life, then righteousness would indeed have been based on law."

If there was any way that people could have been saved by keeping the law in their own strength, God would have done that, but because of Adam's sin, that was now impossible. Salvation by grace, through faith in Christ, was the only way. So, the question stands. Why in the world did God spend so much time detailing laws to obey in the Mosaic covenant if it was never meant to save anyone by their own law-keeping? It seems so confusing!

"But Scripture has shut up all men under sin, that the promise by faith in Jesus Christ might be given to those who believe" (Gal 3:22). As we have said before, the moral law of God has been written on human hearts since the beginning of time. Romans 5:13–14 makes clear that though the moral law had not been clearly written down before the Mosaic covenant, men were still held accountable for it. The main way we know this is true is that death reigned over humanity from the time of Adam until the time of Moses. They knew the law internally, broke it, were held responsible by God, and thus died for their sins. All those humans were following in the footsteps of their forefather Adam in breaking the moral law of God and breaking the covenant of works and thus receiving the penalty of death.

In the Mosaic covenant God wrote down the moral law in stone, literally. He made it much clearer and more obvious. He was trying to more fully convince humanity that there was no way they could ever be saved through law-keeping. Maybe when the law was unclear, intuitive, and murky, written on men's hearts, men might understandably think, "Well, maybe if I'm good enough, I can earn salvation by works." But once it was written so clearly and starkly by Moses in Exodus through Deuteronomy, there was no more excuse for such absurdity. A book titled *The Marrow of Modern Divinity* teaches that "the Lord gave them this law, to the intent they might see how far short they came of yielding that obedience which is therein required, and so, consequently, how sinful they were."[3]

Ultimately the Mosaic covenant is an extension of the covenant of grace. But it uses the covenant of works and the moral law of God to drive men away from their own efforts to be saved and to Christ for salvation. It humbles our self-righteousness and then lifts us out of ourselves by grace alone.

3. Fisher, *Marrow*, 321.

John Piper is helpful as well on this topic. Commenting on Rom 3:19–20, he says, "One of the purposes of God in dealing with Israel the way he did for two thousand years was to show that not only could Israel not be saved through law-keeping, but how much less could anybody else in the world be saved, who didn't have the privileges of Israel. All of this was preparatory for the coming of the Savior, Jesus Christ."[4]

The goal is to humble humanity, to break us of our stubborn pride and self-righteousness. God wants to fully drive his people away from the arrogance of thinking we may ever be good enough to earn our way to heaven. God wants to drive us from our man-made righteousness to flee to Christ alone for salvation.

Application

God's good promises to his people are so good that sometimes they can go to our heads and make us take them for granted. God chose to start his salvation project with Abraham's family, which grew into the nation of Israel. They were not better than other nations, but God's choice at times led many of them to assume that they were inherently better than others. Imagine you and three friends murdered someone and were on death row in prison. I was the governor and came personally to pardon all four of you. Imagine I had two sets of keys to open prison doors. I opened your cell first and then gave you my extra set of keys so you could help me set your friends free more quickly.

Now imagine that your freedom, which preceded theirs, went to your head. Rather than using the keys to set your friends free, you began to strut in front of them and boast of your freedom. You looked down on their continued imprisonment. You felt pride in your newfound freedom. This would be both stupid and arrogant because you had done nothing to deserve your freedom or my choice to open your cell before the cells of your friends. But these blessings went to your head. You misinterpreted them as a sign that you were superior to your friends for something in yourself.

In an analogous way, God's choice of the Jews as his starting point for salvation went to their heads. They looked down on the surrounding nations. They boasted as if they held special merits of their own. They needed to be humbled. John Calvin teaches, "The Jews, puffed up with the privilege

4. Piper, "Why Is Witchcraft," para. 8.

which God had conferred upon them, reckoned the Gentiles to be unworthy of being admitted to any intercourse whatever."[5]

Edward Fisher, the author of *The Marrow of Modern Divinity*, is extremely helpful on this point:

> Their fall in Adam was almost forgotten . . . in that long course of time betwixt Adam and Moses, men had forgotten what was sin; so, although God had made a promise of blessing to Abraham, and to all his seed, that would plead interest in it, yet these people at this time were proud and secure, and heedless of their estate; and though "sin was in them, and death reigned over them" yet they being without a law to evidence this sin . . . unto their consciences, they did not impute it unto themselves, they would not own it, nor charge themselves with it; and so, by consequence, found no need of pleading the promise made to Abraham; (Rom. 5:20), therefore, "the law entered," that Adam's offence and their own actual transgression might abound, so that now the Lord saw it needful, that there should be a new edition and publication of the covenant of works.[6]

Thomas Boston, in a sidenote in Fisher's work, explains further that "the remaining impressions of the law on their hearts were so weak, that they were not sufficient for the purpose."[7] The moral law was written on Adam's heart, but after his fall it was dim and unclear. As hundreds of years of human history passed, though the law remained on humanity's hearts, it became dull and less powerful in conviction.

When God made covenant with Abraham and his descendants, the covenant of grace went to their head. They assumed they were right with God. They didn't humble themselves. They didn't repent. They didn't cling to God and his promises desperately by faith because they didn't feel the need to. The conviction of sin was so light and weak. For this reason, God added the Mosaic law to make the moral law bright and clear and powerful for conviction again. He did this to humble his people out of their pride and self-righteousness and drive them back to him by grace alone.

This can happen to any of us, in any day and country. It happened to Jewish leaders in the days of John the Baptist. He rebuked them, saying, "Do not suppose that you can say to yourselves, 'We have Abraham as our father'" (Matt 3:9). They assumed they were right with God, not because of

5. Calvin, *Commentaries on the Epistles*, 236.

6. Fisher, *Marrow*, 83.

7. Fisher, *Marrow*, 83.

a saving faith relationship but just because they were ethnically Jewish. You see the same attitude in John 8:39 in their debates with Jesus. Their attitude was, "We are the good guys by birth right." They were wrong.

This is how Paul grew up in many ways. In Rom 7:7–13 he shares part of his psychological testimony. Paul says he had the law, but the law did not have him. He grew up in a deeply religious, Jewish household and would have had much of the Mosaic law memorized. He knew it well intellectually, but he experienced no real conviction. He makes a radical statement in Rom 7:9: "I was once alive apart from the Law; but when the commandment came, sin became alive, and I died." Now what does that mean?

Imagine this scenario. A young boy grows up today in the best family, church, and community you can imagine. He is as innocent as he can be at the human level. Obviously, he is a sinner before God, but humanly speaking, he is the greatest child alive. He knows the Ten Commandments, including the commandment not to covet.

Then one day he realizes his friend is a much better athlete than he is. He begins to covet his friend's natural ability. Quickly he realizes this is wrong. But it is not so easy to stop. The sin seems to grow inside of his heart. Conviction comes with guilt and shame.

This young man grew up with the law in his mind. But the law did not seem to be alive with convicting power in his soul until he was clearly found to be in obvious sin. Many of us have had such experiences with different sins.

When Paul says that he was alive apart from the law, he doesn't mean he grew up in a family that didn't hear or believe God's word and or the Mosaic law. He means that he felt righteous. He felt holy. He felt just and right with God. Externally he looked good, and he boasted about that. See Phil 3:4–6 for more of his pre-Christ spiritual resume.

When the law came home to him and started to convict him for inward sins like coveting, he was crushed and humbled. "This commandment, which was to result in life, proved to result in death for me" (Rom 7:10). He grew up with the Ten Commandments, including the tenth, which prohibits coveting. He believed that he could gain spiritual life by obeying the law perfectly. But when he was finally convicted of coveting and tried to stop, he started to realize how sinful he was. Then his deadness in sin, which had been there all along, became clear and overwhelming to him.

We don't know when this happened in his life for sure. It seems likely to me that this happened the first time he heard Stephen preach. They were both Greek-speaking Jews who knew the Bible. They had some similarities. They were up-and-coming religious leaders. But no one could refute Stephen's preaching, even the mighty Paul. Paul had been the star student in Judaism, an expert on the Old Testament, until Stephen preached and Paul (then called Saul) was humbled. He coveted Stephen's preaching gifts, his knowledge, and his fame. He couldn't stand to be outdone. So, he consented to kill Stephen. This is when the law began to come home to Paul and crush him with conviction. (For more on this theory, see Gal 1:14 and Acts 6:9–10, 7:2–54, and 8:1).

Why does God do it this way? To expose our sin and to ruin our presumption of self-righteousness. God must humble us out of our pride before he can save us. Martin Luther teaches, "The principal point of the law in true Christian theology is to make men not better, but worse."[8] This is remarkably similar to what Paul says. God uses the law to make our sin clear to us, "that through the commandment sin might become utterly sinful" (Rom 10:13). When anyone genuinely puts their life up against the moral law of God they will be humbled and broken. They will begin to see the depth, the evil, the insanity of their sin.

John Bunyan gives an incredible example of this in his allegory *Pilgrim's Progress*. At the interpreter's house there is a room filled with dust on the floor. Someone tries to sweep all the dust out. But the broom alone actually stirs the dust up to make people in the room choke. Then a little water is sprinkled in the room to settle the dust. Then the broom is used to sweep the dust out of the room without causing those nearby to struggle and cough.

The room represents the human heart dead in sin. The broom represents the moral law of God. The water represents the grace of God. Until someone has experienced the saving grace of God in their life, the moral law will not make them better. In some sense it will make them worse. It will expose their sin. It will stir sinful desires up. It will show them the depth of their depravity and hopefully drive them to their need for Christ and salvation.[9]

Luther goes further: "It is necessary that he should be humbled by the law so that this beast, the presumption of righteousness, might be slain; otherwise, man cannot obtain life. God, seeing that this universal plague of the whole world—that is, man's opinion of his own righteousness, his

8. Luther, *Commentary on Galatians*, 214.

9. Bunyan, *Pilgrim's Progress*, 116–19.

hypocrisy, and confidence in his own holiness—could not be beaten down by any other means, He would that it should be slain by the law."[10]

John Stott quotes Emil Brunner as saying, "To stand on the rim of the abyss, to despair utterly of ever crossing over, this is the indispensable 'antechamber of faith.'"[11] God must bring us to the end of ourselves and our self-righteous hopes before we can accept salvation by faith alone.

The Puritan Richard Sibbes teaches, "None are fitter for comfort than those that think themselves furthest off. Men, for the most part, are not lost enough in their own feeling for a Savior. A holy despair of ourselves is the ground of true hope."[12] It is good to be broken under the convicting power of the law.

John Gerstner says, "Nothing now stands between the sinner and God but the sinner's 'good works.'"[13] If we cling desperately to our own righteous record, we will be damned. If we boast in our own spiritual resume, we cannot have Christ as our Savior, substitute, and sacrifice. God ruins us so he can "righteous" us. God wrecks us so he can redeem us.

Conclusion

My guess is most reading this book know the facts about sin. We are even aware at some level of our own sinfulness. But many of us do not feel the problem. It is far too easy, in a world like ours, to turn on the TV for five minutes and see plenty of examples of people more outwardly sinful than us. We may never say it out loud, but inwardly we can think, "At least I'm not as bad as those people." We often have the heart of the Pharisee: "I thank Thee that I am not like other people" (Luke 18:11).

We say with our mouths boldly, "I'm saved by faith alone!" Yet inwardly in our heart we can feel like the best person alive. This is one reason the comparison game is so deadly. There will always be more scandalous sinners than us. Their existence helps us with our pride.

We subconsciously start to base a tiny bit of our standing on our virtuous deeds. Our sense of self-worth gets tied up in our own effort. When my kids were younger, I often struggled with my anger with them. I was a minister who was thirty-plus years old. They were all sixteen and under at the

10. Luther, *Commentary on Galatians*, 219.

11. Stott, *Romans*, 118.

12. Sibbes, *Bruised*, 14.

13. Quoted in Keller, *Romans*, 38.

time. Yet I could find myself justifying myself in my mind: "They started it. He yelled first." What a sin! What stupidity! What arrogance! What a self-righteous attempt to make myself feel better about myself. What an attempt to distance myself ever so slightly from the depth of my sinful anger.

Why do we do this internally so often, so quickly? We are desperate to hang on to some shred of self-righteousness. We want so much to have a little bit of spiritual dignity for ourselves. It hurts to say, "I am a wretched sinner, worthy of hell, saved only by grace and mercy." There is a part of me to this day that truly hates to confess the depths of my ongoing indwelling sin.

Tim Keller wisely instructs, "'good deeds' done outside of the gospel make your soul go sour."[14] Have you experienced this? To the degree you base your sense of self-worth on your personal goodness you will be cursed. If you think you're doing better than most you will be arrogant and stuck up. To the degree you think you're failing and sinning you will be depressed and miserable. Only when we can say, "My righteousness is the righteousness of Christ," can we truly be free forever from the sinful comparison game.

Salvation by grace alone frees us from arrogance and from sinful self-hatred and loathing. We don't really believe what Jesus taught in Matt 5. At heart, we are all murderers. We all have the potential to be the next Hitler if left to ourselves.

This can seem like so much sad news that it is depressing. How can these truths be part of the good news message? Imagine walking on the beach with a friend and cutting your toe on a shell. It bled a little and your friend just happened to have a Band-Aid. You put on the Band-Aid, and it protects your cut toe from hurting as you walk. You thank your friend. Maybe you give him a grateful fist bump and a smile.

Imagine the same scenario except this time a tsunami wave comes in, sucks you out to sea, and drowns you. Your friend courageously swims to save you, drags you to shore, and gives you CPR. He restores you to life. But he is so exhausted from all the Herculean effort that he dies on the spot from a heart attack. What level of gratitude would you feel at this moment? A smile, a word, and a fist bump would never suffice.

You would feel such a wealth of gratitude welling up in your soul. You would be moved to dedicate the rest of your life to honoring such a friend.

14. Keller, *Romans*, 37.

If he had a family, you would want to do all you could to serve them out of love for your savior.

Imagine a group of basketball players that played together all four years of high school together. They lost every game for four straight years. Their senior year, they barely won the last game of the year. How might they respond? They'd go nuts in celebration. They were so used to defeat; they now much more deeply relished the thrill of victory at last.

If we have a small view of our sin, we will have a small view of our Savior and thus our joy in him will be small. If we minimize our sinful condition, we will end up necessarily minimizing the greatness of our salvation. We will treat Jesus like a friend with a Band-Aid for our toe. We will treat him like one more small victory in life to celebrate.

The more we are honest and realistic about our own ongoing sin, the deeper our joy will be in the fact that Christ has saved us from it. We were drowning in the guilt, shame, and bondage of our sin. But Christ gave his life to swim into the wrath of God and bring us safe to shore. When we see how dead we were in sin before trusting in him, we will rejoice so much more in him. We will long so much more to live for him.

"And the Law came in that the transgression might increase; but where sin increased, grace abounded all the more, that, as sin reigned in death, even so grace might reign through righteousness to eternal life through Jesus Christ our Lord" (Rom 5:20–21). Richard Sibbes teaches, "There is more mercy in Christ than sin in us."[15]

Jesus taught, "He who is forgiven little, loves little" (Luke 7:47). None of us is forgiven little. But some in our arrogance and ignorance think we have been forgiven little, and thus our love for Christ is often cold and timid. The more we can let the law have its way with us, the more we will be delighted in such great salvation. Let the law humble, break, and convict you to your core. Then rise in rejoicing for such a great Savior.

John Newton was an evil slave trader that Christ saved. He grew into a wonderful pastor and hymn writer, writing the most well-known hymn of all time, "Amazing Grace." Late in life, near death, he lost much of his memory. But his famous last words are powerful. "I am a great sinner but Christ is a great Savior."[16] This is the truth of the gospel for any one of us in Christ. Hallelujah! What a Savior.

15. Sibbes, *Bruised*, 13.

16. Koukl, "Telling Parting Words," para. 3.

Chapter 5

Jesus Fulfills the Law

When God gave the Law to Moses in the Mosaic covenant, he gave it in three parts. First, and primarily, there was the moral law. The moral law is most clearly summarized in the Old Testament with the Ten Commandments. But as we have said before, the moral law has always existed. It is a righteous revelation of the heart and character of God. It was written on mankind's heart from the beginning of creation. It remains in men's hearts today even though it is cracked and unclear because of our sin nature.

The first part of the Ten Commandments, the first four commandments, deal with our relationship with God. They explain what it looks like to love the Lord our God. The second part of the commandments, the last six, deal with our relationship with other humans. They explain what it means to love our neighbor as ourselves.

But God did not only give the moral law in the Mosaic covenant. He also gave the ceremonial law and the civil law. The ceremonial and civil were added to the moral law and were always meant to be temporary, for certain people at a certain time in a certain place. The ceremonial law told ancient Israel how to rightly love and worship the one true God in very practical and tangible ways. The civil law told the Old Testament people of God how to properly love one another and all other humans in that day and age and setting.

When you read the books of Moses in the Old Testament, (Exodus, Leviticus, Numbers, and Deuteronomy) there are not crystal-clear division between these three sections of the law at all times. They are often jumbled together. Why has God done it this way? What was he doing when he added these two other sections to the already existing moral law of God?

God was seeking to give the budding nation of Israel crystal-clear directives for what his moral law meant for them: as the ancient people of God, how should they love God and neighbor? He was trying to spell out for them in their very specific context how to love God and how to love others. He was giving them very tangible and easily understandable directives about how the moral law of God should be applied in their local, agrarian society.

The people of God in the Old Testament were in spiritual infancy. This is part of what Paul means when he says "we were kept in custody under the law, being shut up to the faith which was later to be revealed. Therefore the Law has become our tutor to lead us to Christ, that we may be justified by faith" (Gal 3:22–24).

When your kids are young and immature you give very specific directions: "You may go outside and play in our yard with your friends. Do not leave our yard. Stay where you can hear my voice if I walk outside and call your name. Be nice. Don't get into fights. Be ready to come in when the sun starts to set for dinner." But when our children are older and more mature, we tend to give them the important principles but much more freedom in application: "Sure, you can go hang out with your friends. Just please be safe and be home by midnight." In the Old Testament, under the Mosaic law, the people of God (called the nation of Israel) were spiritually young and immature and needed lots of specifics. Hence the ceremonial and civil law were added to the moral law. Now, in Christ, maturity has come to God's people in general, compared with the Old Testament believers. God's focus is more on principles and less on applications in the New Testament. The moral law still stands for us. The civil and the ceremonial laws do not still apply to us.

For example, Exod 20:17 is part of the moral law, the Ten Commandments. Paul mentions this specific commandment in Rom 7 as we saw in the last chapter. Notice the specificity of the commandment as far as the local context. "You shall not covet your neighbor's house; you shall not covet your neighbor's wife or his male servant or his female servant or his ox or his donkey or anything that belongs to your neighbor" (Exod 20:17). This is a timeless commandment for all people, including Paul living and writing Romans after the resurrection of Christ. Yet, it's highly likely Paul didn't own an ox or a donkey or have any servants. Most of us reading this book may have a house and a spouse. Most of us likely do not own a donkey or ox. Some of us may have never even seen an ox in real life! So why get so specific about this timeless truth? God was trying to make it very timely, clear, and obvious to the original hearers. He wanted there to be no excuse for a lack of understanding.

If you drop down in Exod 20, just seven verses later, in the same chapter, we get this command. "You shall make an altar of earth for Me, and you shall sacrifice on it your burnt offerings and your peace offerings, your sheep and your oxen" (Exodus 20:24). Again, most of us have never built an altar much less offered sacrifice on it. We're probably not sure of the difference between burnt and peace offerings. Most of us don't own sheep and oxen. Why the specificity? God was giving them a very clear application of how to worship God, how to serve God and honor God in that Old Testament context. Exodus 20:17 is part of the moral law of God. It is still a sin for you and me to covet anything of our neighbor's. Exodus 20:24 is part of the ceremonial law. The ceremonial law told ancient Israelites how to worship and love Yahweh appropriately. It no longer applies to us, or at least not in the same way, as we will show in this chapter. Although the principle of worshiping God remains, the application of building an altar of earth doesn't remain.

Four verses later we come to Exod 21:2. (Remember that chapter and verse distinctions were not in the original text. They were added later for easy reference.) It says, "If you buy a Hebrew slave, he shall serve for six years; but on the seventh he shall go out as a free man without payment." This was part of the civil law. This type of "slavery" allowed in the Old Testament law was an indentured servitude. But God was giving an ancient people who were all too familiar with slavery rules to regulate this servitude so that it did not become abusive. My guess is none of us reading this today have or want an indentured servant. The civil law was God's specific application of the second half of the Ten Commandments to his ancient people.

Imagine I left my oldest son to babysit my younger kids. I told him the rules for the night were very simple and ought to be obvious: "Honor your mom and dad in all you do and love your little siblings in all you say and do." But I might go further and give him some specific examples so there can be no room for doubt or uncertainty. I might say, "Buddy, here's what I practically mean. Obey me while I'm gone as far as what you know I would like you to watch on TV and what I don't want you to be watching. And love your siblings practically by being kind and gentle with them. Don't yell at them or hit them." What have I done?

I started by giving him the overarching principles, the moral law of our household. Then I gave him practical examples of how it should play out in his life that night. That is what God did with the Mosaic covenant and the threefold division of the law. The moral law is made up of the overarching, timeless principles of God's universe. The ceremonial law is the practical examples, so to speak, of how to apply the first four commandments on loving God in their ancient society with the tabernacle and temple, etc. The civil law is clarity for an agrarian society on how to love one another well in all different sorts of specific contexts they might find themselves in.

Thus, the ceremonial law is filled with descriptions of things like how to eat in a certain way to remain separate from pagans who don't worship God. The civil law is filled with directives on ancient punishments if you sinned against your neighbor by stealing and how much you would have to pay them back, etc. Israel in the Old Testament was the people of God in infancy. So, God spelled it out for them, somewhat like we do for young kids. They needed extra clarity. These laws in the Mosaic books can seem all jumbled together but there are clear distinctions.

How can we know that the moral law is still applicable and the ceremonial and civil are not? In one sense, that is the whole question this book seeks to answer, so keep reading and bear with me! But for now, it may be helpful to remember a couple of clear points. Only the Ten Commandments were literally written by God himself. Only the Ten Commandments were written in stone. Only the Ten Commandments were put into the Ark of the Covenant (Exod 24:12 and 25:16). Even in the Old Testament it should have been clear that the moral law contained in the Ten Commandments was unique and greatly superior to the civil and ceremonial law. Being carved in stone by the finger of God is a wonderful way to make the point that the moral law is timeless.[1]

For the purposes of this chapter our main goal is to understand how Christ interacted with this threefold law and, more importantly, how he fulfilled it for his people. At the beginning of the Sermon on the Mount when Christ spoke to a Jewish audience, he said, "Do not think that I came to abolish the Law or the Prophets; I did not come to abolish, but to fulfill. For truly I say to you, until heaven and earth pass away, not the smallest letter or stroke shall pass away from the Law, until all is accomplished" (Matt 5:17–18). Those listening to Christ would have naturally and rightly understood Christ to be speaking of the entire Old Testament, including

1. For more on this see Ferguson, *Whole*, 149–52.

the moral, ceremonial, and civil law of the Mosaic covenant, when he spoke of "the Law and the Prophets." How did Christ fulfill the law in its entirety?

Moral Law

Christ did everything a godly Jew was supposed to do. He did it perfectly, fully, without one ounce of sin. He was not tainted by sinfulness in any way although he was tempted in every way as we are (Heb 4:15). Matthew 4:1–10 and Luke 4:1–13 show Christ at the beginning of his ministry alone in the wilderness, being tempted by Satan.

He is tempted in at least three different ways if not more. He is tempted in his physical appetites with hunger and the temptation to break a fast in a time and way his Father did not want him to and for a wrong reason. He was tempted with possessions. Specifically, he was tempted to skip the cross his Father ordained and still gain all the world for himself. He was also tempted with pride, prestige, grasping for glory, fame, and friendships in a selfish, sinful way.

First John 2:16 says, "For all that is in the world, the lust of the flesh and the lust of the eyes and the boastful pride of life, is not from the Father, but is from the world." John teaches that there are three main rivers of sin, so to speak. The lust of the flesh is our physical appetites gone wild, whether that be with food, drink, sex, sleep, drugs, or more. The lust of the eyes has to do with greed, money, possessions—things of which we feel we can never have enough. The boastful pride of life has to do with our sinful ego that wants to take the place of God and be the center of the universe. All different varieties of sinful actions flow from one of these three springs. Christ was tempted in all these ways in the wilderness and throughout his life. We see much more temptation coming to him on the cross specifically. But he was always sinlessly perfect, every second of every day. He never had one sinful desire, one sinful thought, word, deed, or emotion. He was always perfect and pure.

Luke 4:13 says, "And when the devil finished every temptation." The insinuation is that Satan threw all he had at him and none of it worked. It doesn't mean Satan gave up. It just means the end of the battle was already clear. No matter what Satan did, he would always lose when tempting Christ.

Hebrews 4:15 teaches that Jesus was "tempted in all things as we are, yet without sin." What comfort to know that he knows and understands our struggles and temptations. He is our great High Priest!

I heard a helpful illustration once. Imagine if Satan had a dial to turn up the level of temptation each of us suffers. One would be the lowest level of temptation and ten would be the highest level. For most Christians, Satan turns the dial up to one in a certain area and we resist. He may turn it up to two and we start to pray for help. At level three maybe we quote a verse to ourselves. At level four we phone a friend for help. At level five we may give in. Many of us rarely ever experience temptation at the highest level because we give in at some point.

But Jesus never gave in. He withstood all temptations, even at level ten, for thirty-three years of life. He knows what it means to be tempted in the worst ways. He can "sympathize with our weaknesses" (Heb 4:15).

Ceremonial Law

The ceremonial portion of the Mosaic law instructed the infant people of God how to worship God in ancient times. It included all the different types of sacrifices they were supposed to offer God in the tabernacle and later in the temple. On top of that, it included other things such as the food laws and certain laws about their dress, etc. These laws made them ritually clean to appear in the worship service. These laws also helped them stay distinct and unique from the surrounding pagan nations who worshiped false gods and had different practices. Certain types of foods, feasts, rituals, and clothing were often involved in different types of pagan worship.

In Ephesians, Paul speaks to gentiles (non-Israelites) who had become Christians. He speaks of the times before Christ came saying, "remember that at that time you were separate from Christ, excluded from the commonwealth of Israel, and strangers to the covenants of promise, having no hope and without God in the world" (Eph 2:12). After the time of Abraham, there is no record that God worked savingly in the world anywhere outside of the Jewish nation until Christ came. God gave his covenant and promises to Abraham and his family, the Jews. Only they had hope to know God and be saved. Gentiles could be saved but they would have to encounter a Jew or Jewish writings to then know the Jewish God. Rahab in Josh 2 and 6 is a great example of such a salvation. Jonah, a Jewish prophet, had to be sent to the pagan city Nineveh for them to hear the word of God.

Even if a gentile did trust in Yahweh in the Old Testament, they would not have full rights of access in the Jewish temple. They could enter the court of the gentiles but not into the innermost parts of the temple. But now, in Christ, things have gloriously changed. There was always a distinction between Jew and gentile, even in worship. The ceremonial laws of worship and ritual purity made this distinction exceedingly clear.

> But now in Christ Jesus, you who formerly were far off have been brought near by the blood of Christ. For He Himself is our peace, who made both groups into one, and broke down the barrier of the dividing wall, by abolishing in His flesh the enmity, which is the Law of commandments contained in ordinances, that in Himself He might make the two into one new man, thus establishing peace, and might reconcile them both in one body to God through the cross, by it having put to death the enmity. (Eph 2:13–16)

Christ was a Jew born under the time of the ceremonial law. He kept the ceremonial law perfectly. He fulfilled it. He brought an end to the ceremonial law. Christ ended all religious and spiritual distinctions between Jew and gentile. We can and should be one in Christ when we both trust in him. Our worship and fellowship should be united!

Matthew Henry, a Puritan commentator, says about this passage, "He destroyed the barrier, the ceremonial law, called the dividing wall by way of allusion to the barrier in the temple, which separated the court of the Gentiles from that into which the Jews only had liberty to enter. . . . He took away the binding power of the ceremonial law, the law with its commandments and regulations."[2] Henry is careful to note that Christ did not destroy all of God's law. He did not destroy the moral law at all. He destroyed the ceremonial law. He destroyed them by fulfilling them!

So, now when you read ancient food laws in the Old Testament, you do not have to obey them. Go ahead and have a pork sandwich with a clear conscience! If you want to take personal applications from the ancient food laws because you think it's physically healthier to not eat pork, you are fine to do so. But there is absolutely no sin at all in breaking Mosaic food laws today. They were a part of the ceremonial law that has been fulfilled and thus brought to an end. Mark 7:19 clearly states, "He declared all foods clean."

John Calvin, commenting on Eph 2:14–15, agrees with this perspective. "The ceremonies, by which the distinction was declared, have been

2. Henry, *NIV Matthew Henry Commentary*, 664.

abolished through Christ. What were circumcision, sacrifices, washings, and abstaining from certain kinds of food, but symbols of sanctification, reminding the Jews that their lot was different from that of other nations; . . . Paul is here treating exclusively of the ceremonial law; for the moral law is not a wall of partition separating us from the Jews."[3] The ceremonial law is fulfilled and finished for all believers. The moral law remains.

Christ ultimately fulfilled the ceremonial law by offering the one true necessary sacrifice that all the other sacrifices pointed to.

> When Christ appeared as a high priest . . . He entered through the greater and more perfect tabernacle, not made with hands, that is to say, not of this creation; and not through the blood of goats and calves, but through his own blood, He entered the holy place once for all, having obtained eternal redemption. . . . Christ did not enter a holy place made with hands . . . but into heaven itself, now to appear in the presence of God for us; nor was it that He should offer Himself often, as the high priest enters the holy place year by year with blood not his own . . . but now once at the consummation of the ages He has been manifested to put away sin by the sacrifice of Himself. . . . By this will we have been sanctified through the offering of the body of Jesus Christ once for all. (Heb 9:11–12, 24–26; 10:10)

Old Testament priests went into the tabernacle and then later the temple once it was built. They went year after year repeatedly, offering the blood of animals. The blood of animals cannot save anyone. The blood of Christ can. Christ entered the true tabernacle, heaven itself, the very throne room of God. He took not the blood of bulls or goats, but his very own blood. With his blood he fulfilled all the ceremonial law and purchased redemption for all of his people once and for all!

The Westminster Confession is very helpful on this point. WCF 19.3 states, "God was pleased to give to the people of Israel—as the church in a preparatory stage of development—various ceremonial laws which contained types of things to come. Some of these laws were rites of worship prefiguring Christ, his graces, actions, sufferings and benefits, and others instructed in moral duties. All these ceremonial laws are now discontinued by virtue of the new covenant." Notice, the nation of Israel is considered the immature church, "the church in a preparatory stage." Also notice that the ceremonial laws primarily prefigured Christ. Thus, now that Christ has

3. Calvin, *Commentaries on the Epistles*, 237–38.

come in flesh and blood, the signpost pointing to his coming is no longer necessary.

Civil Law

Lastly, Christ was born in the nation of Israel and lived as a citizen of that earthly nation, even as it was under Roman rule. He was the perfect citizen. He broke no Jewish civil law.

The worst punishment the Mosaic civil law could give was execution. "And if a man has committed a sin worthy of death, and he is put to death, and you hang him on a tree, his corpse shall not hang all night on the tree, but you shall surely bury him on the same day (for he who is hanged is accursed of God)" (Deut 21:22–23). Christ committed no crime worthy of death. He committed no sin worthy of death. Yet he died for all the crimes against God and humans that his people have committed and continue to commit.

The letter of Hebrews was originally written to Jewish Christians in the first century. Notice what the author says: "For here we do not have a lasting city, but we are seeking the city which is to come" (Heb 13:14). Even then, the Christians knew that earthly Jerusalem was no longer their true, lasting city. Their Jewish citizenship and ethnicity were not what mattered. The old Mosaic civil law may have wisdom today for modern governmental laws. But the old Mosaic civil law holds no more authority for God's people today.[4] It was a specific law for a specific group of people in a specific time and place. There is no country on earth today that has the exact same theocratic relationship that Israel did in the Old Testament. God did something very singular and unique with and for ancient Israel. There is no implication that modern nations should try to recreate the same situation.

The Confession is helpful again. WCF 19.4 says, "God also gave to the people of Israel laws to govern them as a nation, and these came to an end with the theocracy. These judicial laws are not obligatory on any other people now except to the extent that general principles of justice and right incorporated in them may require." A theocracy is a nation-state that is set up to be directly run by a deity. The nation of Israel was a theocracy and God wanted it to be that way. That is no longer the case. God doesn't want his people to live in a national theocracy currently. Rather, the New Testament church transcends all nations, borders, and territories. People

4. Ferguson, *Whole*, 145, 152.

from every tongue, tribe, nation, language, and ethnicity will dwell in the new Jerusalem in the next life. Therefore, we can still learn wisdom from the Old Testament in setting up modern day laws. But we are not obliged to keep all of them exactly.

In Israel, in the Old Testament, adultery was punishable by death (Lev 20:10). The Bible does not teach that we must have that as a civil law in our country today. But the New Testament does teach that if someone commits adultery and refuses to repent, they should be excommunicated from church membership (1 Cor 5:1–11). Many of the principles in the civil law can and should be applied in new ways in the New Testament church. This is one example.

For the sake of this chapter, it is important to see that Christ was born under that civil Jewish law as a Jewish citizen. He obeyed it perfectly. He has fulfilled that part of the law for us as well. He fulfilled it in his life and in his death.

Application

Have you ever wondered why Christ was born as an infant and then lived thirty-three years? In fact, most of his first thirty years were lived in obscurity with only three years of public ministry at the end. Why not come to earth as the God-man on a Friday? He could teach, preach, heal, and cast out many demons before being arrested and crucified. Sunday he could rise from the dead. The gospel accomplished in a weekend!

At least one of the reasons for him living on earth over three decades was that he could live a full, complete, human life. He lived the life under the Mosaic law that a Jew in that age was supposed to live. More importantly, he lived under the covenant of works that we are all supposed to live. But none of us can live that life. None of us have.

We are all born under the covenant of works. We have all broken the covenant of works. We are all doomed to die and suffer hell eternally under the covenant of works.

The Mosaic covenant spelled out the covenant of works in more detail than any other covenant. There is a sense, under it, that all of us would be guilty of death before God. We are all murderers and adulterers at heart according to the teaching of Christ in Matt 5. We all deserve to hang on a cross under the wrath of God. We deserve to be abandoned. We have clearly merited hell with our ongoing sinfulness and rebellion.

Apart from Christ, Gal 3:10 applies to us all: "For as many as are of the works of the Law are under a curse; for it is written, 'Cursed is everyone who does not abide by all things written in the book of the law, to perform them.'" We all rightly deserve eternal damnation for all our sin. The main application is to despair of your own righteousness and look away from yourself. Despair of all hope in yourself and look for a Savior!

Conclusion

"But when the fulness of the time came, God sent forth His Son, born of a woman, born under the Law, in order that He might redeem those who were under the Law, that we might receive, the adoption as sons. . . . Therefore you are no longer a slave, but a son; and if a son, then an heir through God" (Gal 4:4–5, 7).

We are all born under the moral law of God as a covenant. We are all born dead in our sins, under the covenant of works. We therefore can only relate to God as a slave. It is a hopeless situation if we are left alone.

But Christ, the one true Son of God, willingly gave up many of the experiences of his sonhood for a time, for us. He was born under moral law, under the covenant of works. He obeyed it perfectly. He should have come to the end of his life and been commended by all! Rather he was cursed in my place and in your place if you have trusted him (Gal 3:13).

Maybe the greatest gospel summary ever is 2 Cor 5:21, which says, "He made Him who knew no sin to be sin on our behalf, that we might become the righteousness of God in Him." God the Father made Christ the Son to be our substitute for our sin. He died in our place. But he also lived in our place. He lived the perfect life we are supposed to live but cannot. He died the horrible judicial death we deserve to die but don't want to. No one wants to suffer and die under the wrath of God and be forsaken by him.

By his great grace and mercy, we can live. We can be free. We can be forgiven. We can relate to God as Father and not as a slave master anymore.

You may know all the right gospel answers. But has the gospel truly sunk into the basement of your heart? Do you know God personally as your Father? Do you experience him that way?

In your time of prayer and throughout the day, how do you honestly relate to God? Is there freedom, joy, and confidence that accords with adoption? Or is there fear and terror and shrinking back that acts as though you are still under his wrath?

Are you subtly trying to work to earn something from him with your good work? Or do you genuinely believe Jesus has already earned it all for you, in your place? "Jesus paid it all, / All to him I owe; / Sin had left a crimson stain, / He washed it white as snow."[5]

When it comes to our relationship with God, Christians should honestly take the words "earn," "deserve," and "merit" out of our vocabulary. They have no place in that relationship anymore. We relate to God based on sheer grace, secured for us by Christ.

I took one of my sons on a ski trip when he was twelve. The purpose was primarily to have fun with him and show him how much I loved him. We had a lot of fun, ate great food, and spent a lot of money! At the end of the trip, my son woke up early on his own accord. He cleaned the room we were staying in. He took out the trash and fixed breakfast for me. When I got out of bed he said, "Dad, I wanted to clean the room and fix breakfast just to say thanks for this great trip!"

He wasn't trying to earn anything. The gift had already been given. The relationship was well established. Why had he woken up early to work hard and clean the room, etc.? He was grateful. He was happy. He felt love towards me for the great gift I had given him.

In a very similar way, this is how believers should obey our Father in heaven. There should be a sense of joy, gladness, gratitude, and even awe. A great gift has already been purchased. We didn't have to pay. Christ paid with his blood. We are free. We are forgiven. We are adopted. We are secure. We should thus be motivated to now obey the moral law from a place of freedom. We don't have to obey it perfectly; Christ has already done that for us. We are free to stumble forward and by grace attempt to obey it from a place of love and gratitude. "Amazing love! How can it be / That Thou, my God, should die for me?"[6]

5. Hall, "Jesus Paid It All."

6. Wesley, "And Can It Be?"

Chapter 6

The End of the Mosaic Covenant

A BRIEF REVIEW WILL be helpful at this point. Adam was created and immediately brought into a covenant of works with God. If Adam had obeyed perfectly, he would have lived eternally and been blessed with no interruptions.

Adam chose to sin. All people sinned and fell with him in that original sin because he was our representative, our federal head. All humanity was in Adam's loins, to use the language of Heb 7:10. Romans 1 teaches that all people have some knowledge of this, some sense of this in their heart, even if they are deeply suppressing this truth.

All people from Adam until now are brought into the world under that covenant of works. All people are dead in their sins from the moment of conception because of the original fall in Adam. There is no hope for any sinner to be saved by the covenant of works because the requirement is sinless perfection.

God also made a covenant of grace with Adam starting in Gen 3 after the fall into sin. If Adam trusted God and his promise of a coming Messiah, he would be saved. This covenant of grace was clarified and made more explicit in the covenant God made with Abraham.

God also made a covenant with the nation of Israel during the time of Moses. God set forth the covenant of works and the covenant of grace side by side in the Mosaic covenant. The Mosaic covenant highlighted and emphasized the law of God to humble people and drive them to the covenant of grace.

The Mosaic law had three parts: moral, ceremonial, and civic. Christ was born under the covenant of works and under the Mosaic law. He fulfilled all three parts of the Mosaic law and the covenant of works perfectly. He did this in the place of his people. Anyone who trusts in Christ as their saving substitute will be saved.

This brings us to the question for this chapter. What is the role of the Mosaic law and the Mosaic covenant today? We will primarily look at a passage in Galatians to help us address this.

It's helpful to remember that in the first century most Christians were Jewish. Many of them still went to the temple to pray if they lived in Jerusalem before the temple was destroyed by the Romans. Christianity is the proper fulfillment of biblical Judaism.

Many gentiles began to be saved through the missionary efforts of people like Paul and Barnabas. This reality caused trouble for the first-century church. Acts 15:1–10 highlights these issues in discussing what is commonly called the Jerusalem council. As many gentiles were converted, it forced the apostles and elders to wrestle with the issue of how much, if any, of the Mosaic covenant and law gentile converts must keep.

There was a group of professing Christian teachers commonly called the Judaizers. Paul refers to this group in Gal 2:12 as "the party of the circumcision." They taught that gentile converts had to be circumcised to be saved. They believed and taught that gentiles must keep the law of Moses. See Acts 15:1–5 for more on this.

Galatians was written to confront this heresy. In Paul's letter he explains the gospel clearly. Galatians 3:17 is a verse we've already examined in this book. The Mosaic law came hundreds of years after God's clear covenant of grace based on God's promise to Abraham. The Mosaic law was never intended by God in any way to lessen or threaten the promise of free grace God gave to Abraham and those to come after him. Paul has three things to say about the Mosaic law that we will examine in this chapter. He teaches that Mosaic law is a *tutor*, that it is *temporary*, and that it is *terminated.*

Tutor

Galatians 3:23 can be hard to understand and interpret at first: "But before faith came, we were kept in custody under the law, being shut up to the faith which was later to be revealed." Paul is not implying that faith wasn't operating in the Old Testament. He is not teaching that people were saved in the Old Testament by works and that faith had no place. This would clearly contradict the clear teaching of Gen 15:6 that Abraham was saved by faith: "Then he believed in the LORD; and He reckoned it to him as righteousness."

What he does mean is that the Mosaic covenant tended to put the spotlight more on God's law rather than on faith. John 1:17 is very helpful in this discussion: "For the Law was given through Moses; grace and truth were realized through Jesus Christ." What does John mean?

Again, it's impossible to say that John means that there was no truth and no grace before Jesus Christ came to earth. If that were true, he would be saying the entire Old Testament wasn't true! Obviously, that is not true! This is not what he means.

What he means is that the emphasis of so much of the Mosaic covenant was the law. The law was pushed to the forefront and highlighted to humble men. But once Christ has come, law fades to the background in a sense. Now the spotlight is on grace. The truth is seen more clearly and fully. Augustine famously taught that "truth . . . veiled in the Old Testament, is revealed in the New."[1]

The Mosaic law and covenant were like guards that held and protected the nation of Israel. Remember the nation of Israel in the Old Testament was the church, the people of God, but in an infant stage. The Mosaic law and covenant helped prepare the ancient, infant people of God to prepare to grow into an adult church and people of God.

Imagine you leave an inheritance for your grandchildren. But as you write your will, your grandchildren are all still in diapers. They are nowhere near ready to handle the responsibility that comes with inheriting large amounts of money and property. How would you handle such a situation? You would likely put the money into a trust so that the children could not fully access the money until they are twenty-five years old and their brains have fully developed. You may put a guardian in charge of the trust until they are twenty-five to manage the money in the meantime. God had great things planned and prepared for his people in the Old Testament, but they weren't mature enough yet to handle the full burden of the blessings.

Paul teaches that the Mosaic "Law has become our tutor to lead us to Christ" (Gal 3:24). A tutor in the first century Roman Empire was not like a tutor today. Today a tutor is often a college student. You pay $20 an hour so the tutor will help your high schooler with their math homework and preparing for the ACT. Back then, a tutor was more of a guardian and

1. Augustine, *City*, 171.

babysitter of sorts. Rich families would hire a "tutor" as a nanny in a sense. The tutor's job was to make sure the child arrived at school on time. The tutor might stay at the school in the classroom. If the student did not pay attention to the teacher, the tutor might discipline the child. The tutor was essentially a custodian to take the child to school, protect them, and discipline them.

This is what the Mosaic law was doing for believers in the Old Testament. It helped keep the nation of Israel close to God even when they had only a dim understanding of the covenant of grace. The Mosaic covenant was also preparing them to receive Christ as Messiah when he finally came.

When Jesus first arrived on the scene, John the Baptist proclaimed, "Behold, the Lamb of God who takes away the sin of the world!" (John 1:29). This statement would have made no sense at all if faithful Jews had not have been sacrificing lambs for their sins for hundreds of years. The center point of history was the life, death, and resurrection of Christ in our place, as our sacrificial substitute. It is the most important event in history. It needed a lot of preparation so that it could be rightly understood, appreciated, appropriated, and applied to people's lives correctly.

This work of preparation is what so much of the Mosaic law and covenant was all about. The sacrifices and ceremonies pointed to Christ, prepared people for Christ, and explained Christ. It should have been obvious to devout Jews when he finally came what the reason for his coming was. But the stubbornness and sinfulness of the human heart still blinded so many then and now to the realities of the gospel.

Temporary

Salvation by faith was clear enough in the Old Testament but not as clear as it is in the New Testament. B. B. Warfield, the great Princeton Presbyterian, is helpful: "The Old Testament may be likened to a chamber richly furnished but dimly lighted; the introduction of light brings into it nothing which was not in it before; but it brings out into clearer view much of what is in it but was only dimly or even not at all perceived before. . . . Thus the Old Testament revelation of God is not corrected by the fuller revelation which follows it, but is only perfected, extended and enlarged."[2] New Testament revelation has turned the lights on in a brighter way for us to understand God's word, will, ways, and wisdom.

2. Quoted in Ferguson, *Whole*, 152.

"But now that faith has come, we are no longer under a tutor. For you are all sons of God through faith in Christ Jesus" (Gal 3:25–26). After the resurrection of Christ, God's people no longer live under the Mosaic law or covenant. That tutor is no longer needed because Christ came. You may feel individually like an infant believer at times. (I know that I still do sometimes!) But the New Testament church as a whole, in comparison to the Old Testament church as a whole, is an adult compared to a child. Why is this so? Because the coming of Christ, his life, death, and resurrection are so monumental and effective. The Holy Spirit has now been poured out since Acts 2 in such a new, great, and magnificent way. We are now able to understand so much more of the gospel truth in clarity. We today understand more of the gospel in many ways than men like Moses, David, and Isaiah did.

One of the things that is clearer today than it was three thousand years ago is that all believers are adopted into God's family likes heirs. We don't primarily relate to God as slaves working in his vineyard. Rather, we relate to him primarily as sons, going to work with our daddy!

Jeremiah 31:31–34 speaks to this reality. Believers in the Old Testament were under the covenant of grace. But the covenant of grace was administered through the Mosaic covenant (from Exodus on), which had the Mosaic law spotlighted heavily. New Testament believers are also under the covenant of grace as well, but it is now administered though the new covenant, which Jeremiah prophesied about and Christ sealed with his blood.

Sinclair Ferguson is very helpful on this point:

> Believers have, in redemptive historical terms, transitioned from an era of being heirs but slaves, to a new epoch of being mature sons who enjoy the Spirit of adoption and use Jesus' mode of address to God as they cry, "Abba! Father!" *(No Old Testament believer ever cries, 'Abba! Father!')* . . . Yet this is a comparative antithesis, not an absolute one . . . the Old Testament believer tasted rich blessings within the context of the Mosaic administration. But *by comparison* with the fullness of grace in Christ, they pale into insignificance.[3]

Old Testament believers could see the gospel in a shadowy way. It is as though they had to squint and see it from afar at the first light of day. They could barely discern and understand the contours of the truth that was saving them. In the New Testament, we have been brought close, the lights

3. Ferguson, *Whole*, 148–49.

have been turned on, the sun is high in the sky, there is not a cloud in the sky, all has been made clear! And yet, we know even now, our salvation will be more full, clear, and understandable in the next life when we see Christ face-to-face.

Sacrifices were never meant to cleanse people. They never really could change people and bring forgiveness in and of themselves. The author of Hebrews says as much. When he speaks of the Law, he speaks of the Mosaic covenant.

> For the Law, since it has only a shadow of the good things to come and not the very form of things, can never by the same sacrifices year by year, which they offer continually, make perfect those who draw near. Otherwise, would they not have ceased to be offered, because the worshipers, having once been cleansed, would no longer have had consciousness of sins? . . . For it is impossible for the blood of bulls and goats to take away sins. (Heb 10:1–4)

If the blood of bulls and goats really "worked," they wouldn't have been repeated. Genuine believers in the Old Testament seemed to have consciences continually stained with sin though not oppressed with guilt. This is something the blood of Christ frees us from in the new covenant.

The sacrifices of the Old Testament pointed to Christ continually, which was wonderful. But they also simultaneously pointed back to the sins of the believers continually, which was obviously hard. God was preparing his people for Christ. He was preparing them to fully know him and appreciate him! He wanted them and us to see how radical and how gracious and how powerful his life, death, and resurrection were and are and continue to be for all eternity.

Imagine going to the temple in the Old Testament. So much of the experience would be screaming at you, "You don't belong here! You deserve death!" There was likely the sound of animals being killed, maybe bleating as they died. You would have seen the blood that had been spilled and applied to the altar. You might smell the burning animals on the altar. All of these would have reminded you starkly: "You are a sinner. God is holy and perfect and set apart. You deserve to die. You deserve to have your blood shed. You deserve to be burned up by God's anger. You have no right to be here except by sheer grace and mercy!"

All of this was to lay a foundation so that God's old covenant people (believers before Christ) and new covenant people (believers since Christ) would never forget the holiness of God, his loftiness and transcendence.

God hates sin and wants us to know it fully and remember it. There is an appropriate trembling in his holy presence. He desires us to walk righteously and cautiously before him. Those twin truths should lead us to deep humility and awe and remind us of how great his grace is!

Terminated

Paul teaches, "For Christ is the end of the law for righteousness to everyone who believes" (Rom 10:4). This means two things. First, Christ fulfilled the law for us as we showed in the last chapter.[4] It also means that the law points to Christ as Savior.

Paul further teaches that when someone comes to Christ they are "clothed . . . with Christ" (Gal 3:27). We are justified and declared righteous because we are covered with his righteous record. I am still sinful. I still commit sins. Martin Luther famously said that Christians are simultaneously sinful and righteous.[5]

John Stott says, "Justification is more than forgiveness or acquittal or even acceptance; it is a declaration that we sinners are now righteous in God's sight, because of his conferment upon us of a righteous status, which is indeed the righteousness of Christ himself. . . . He became sin with our sin, so that we might become righteous with his righteousness."[6] This is the greatest news in the world.

Salvation doesn't mean God gave us a blank slate. If that was true, I would dirty the slate again immediately, and so would you. Justification doesn't just mean a second chance. You and I would blow through the next trillion chances God might give us. Justification is a finished work. Christ lived the sinless life under the law as a covenant of works. He lived as a substitute and stood in for all his people, for all time. All the sin of all his people for all times, past, present, and future, were put on Christ on the cross, and he was punished fully for them. So, when we trust in Christ, we are fully free and clear and clean from all spot and blemish in the courtroom of the universe forever! We cannot screw up his work for us. "There is therefore now no condemnation for those who are in Christ Jesus" (Rom 8:1).

The ceremonial law made distinctions between male and female, slave and free, Jew and gentile. For example, men received the sign of the

4. Fisher, *Marrow*, 67, 94.

5. Sproul, "What Does."

6. Stott, *Romans*, 253.

covenant, circumcision, and women did not. What often happens then and now is the people take those distinctions and twist them into something to make them feel better about themselves. They compare themselves to others to feel significant and important. Some Pharisees used to pray, "Thank God I'm not a Gentile, a woman, or a slave."[7]

"There is neither Jew nor Greek, there is neither slave nor free man, there is neither male nor female; for you are all one in Christ Jesus. And if you belong to Christ, then you are Abraham's offspring, heirs according to promise" (Gal 3:28–29). What is Paul saying in these two verses? He is not saying that Jews and Greeks lose their ethnicity. He is not saying that every slave had already been set free physically. Nor was he saying that there were no distinctions whatsoever between men and women. Rather, he is saying that what is most important about us is none of those secondary distinctions. The most important fact about any human is their relationship to Christ.

If someone has trusted in Christ, then they have been forgiven and have become a full and equal heir with him spiritually. That is the greatest significance one can ever hope to attain! And if someone has not trusted in Christ, then no earthly distinction makes them any closer to salvation. The gift comes by grace alone. And when it comes to anyone, it comes full and free.

So, if you are a rich Jewish free man or a poor gentile slave woman it ultimately matters not. One may experience more earthly privileges in the short run. But in the long run, if both trust in Christ, they will be equal eternally. They will rule and reign and rejoice together in the full pardon Christ has purchased for them! The earthly distinctions, privileges, and burdens will fade to the background in heaven. They should begin to fade now in their significance to us.

Application

Why have I chosen to spend so much time on this topic of Mosaic law? There are at least two reasons. First, we need to know how to read the Old Testament and all the laws contained therein. We will continue to talk about moral law further in this book because it predated the Mosaic law. Moral law was functioning in the garden of Eden, and it continues to function in the world today, in your heart and mine. God's law is written on all people's

7. Rowell, "Thank God."

hearts no matter how sketchy their personal awareness of it may be at any given time.

Civil and ceremonial laws are different than moral law. They were specific applications for specific people living in a specific nation at a specific time. That time and nation have passed and so have those laws. Most importantly, Christ was born under the Mosaic law: moral, civil, and ceremonial. And he fulfilled all three components of the law perfectly and precisely.

One example can make this very clear. Since AD 70 there has been no temple or tabernacle in Jerusalem or anywhere else on earth. Read through the book of Leviticus, which is part of the Mosaic law, and see how much of it prescribes how and when and where animal sacrifices were to be offered. That has all been swept away. No temple or tabernacle stands for us to offer sacrifices even if we wanted to. Furthermore, the one true Lamb of God who takes away the sin of the world has already been slain once and for all! All the sacrificial lambs of the Old Testament were mere signposts pointing to him. Now that the reality has come the signs are no longer necessary! Colossians 2:17 teaches that the ceremonial law was a mere shadow. Christ is the substance!

There may be principles of justice and morality we can learn and apply from the civil law of Israel. But we are not supposed to try to reenact their code of justice precisely in our day and age. Westminster Confession of Faith 19.4 states, "God also gave to the people of Israel laws to govern them as a nation and these came to an end with the theocracy. These judicial laws are not obligatory on any other people now except to the extent that general principles of justice and right incorporated in them may require." To the degree that we can discern universal principles of justice in Old Testament law, we should seek to apply those in our modern life. For example, the Mosaic law taught that restitution should be paid when someone was caught stealing. But exactly how much restitution should be repaid can be debated in different scenarios.

The first reason to spend so much time on Mosaic law can feel a little academic at times and may not be as interesting to everyone. But the second one certainly touches us all. The second reason to explain the place of the Mosaic law to such an extent is that all people are tempted at times towards works righteousness. And the Mosaic law can be a useful tool in the hands of Satan to confuse us and draw us away from salvation by faith alone. There's nothing wrong with the law. But as Paul taught in Rom

7:8–11, "sin, taking opportunity through the commandment," can deceive us and produce sin in us.

Conclusion

When an unbeliever truly hears and understands the moral law, it convicts and crushes them. One of God's goals for the law is to drive us to Christ. The law is meant to break us of any hope of works righteousness and thus drive us out of ourselves to the one and only Savior. Paul describes this happening in his life in Rom 7:8–14 and 24–25.

But even after we have trusted in Christ alone for salvation, we need the moral law to continue to humble us and break us and drive us back to Christ afresh. Paul illustrates this happening in his life as a mature believer in Rom 7:15–25. All Christians will struggle at times with some seasons of self-righteousness and at other times we will struggle with insecurity. Often this happens when we compare ourselves to others who may seem to be doing better or worse than us in that moment.

Think about the last time you walked into a crowded room where you did not know many people. Maybe you were attending a business meeting out of town. Maybe you were a new student at school and walked into the cafeteria alone. Maybe you attended a party with your spouse and their friends. When you walk into a room and don't know most people, is there any feeling of insecurity? Is there any sense of scanning the room and comparing yourself to others? I believe there is for most if not all of us.

Most of us survey the crowd and wonder where we fit in the pecking order. We look for something internally to make us feel better about ourselves at that moment. We may look around and feel like we are more physically attractive than most in the room, and this gives us a sense of security. Or we may look around and feel that we are more successful in life and have more money than most in the room. This can give us a sense of well-being. Some of us may compare ourselves to others and rest in our godliness or Bible knowledge. This can make us feel better about ourselves and our standing in the world. But the point is, when we feel weak and insecure in life, we are often tempted to find something about ourselves that makes us feel strong, safe, secure, important, etc. We look for a sense of identity and purpose and meaning. This is not a wrong desire. The problem is that we typically start by looking for these things in the wrong places.

Luke 7:36–47 tells a true story of a self-righteous Pharisee who had some interest in Jesus. He had heard something about this famous teacher, so he invited him over for a meal to evaluate Christ for himself. During the party a sinful woman came in uninvited.

We do not know much about this woman for sure, but it is likely that she was a known sexual sinner. She may have been a prostitute or a known adulteress. The Pharisee knew who she was. She obviously had a bad reputation in town. A party for all the stuck-up self-righteous people in town would be the last place she would want to be. Yet Jesus was there, and she was drawn to him.

She came in as Jesus ate and knelt behind him. She wet his feet with her tears and dried them with her hair. She paid him great honor. It was a lavish display of love. It certainly made those watching uncomfortable, especially the host of the party. This is not what he had envisioned for his party that day.

The Pharisee thought to himself, "If Jesus really knew how sinful this woman really was, he would never let such an unclean woman touch him. He must not really be a prophet." Jesus proved his prophetic gift by reading the Pharisee's mind and responding to his inner thoughts with a story.

He told a story of a person who lent two other people some money. One owed great debt. The second owed a smaller debt. The lender forgave both the debts. Jesus then asked which debtor would love the lender more. The Pharisee correctly answered that the one who had been forgiven the greatest debt would love the forgiver the most.

This Pharisee had been comparing himself to the sinful woman and resting in his smug self-righteousness: "I've never sinned as big and as bad as she has!" Further, he was comparing himself to Jesus and feeling pretty good about himself: "I'm morally clean and very intelligent. This man is supposedly a prophet and doesn't even know the origins of this evil woman he allows to touch him so intimately?!" He has a self-righteous worldview that Christ is about to destroy.

The comparison game is never helpful for our spiritual life. Either we look around and feel worse than others and thus feel despair and self-loathing—this tends to drive us away from others in unhelpful ways—or we compare ourselves to others and for the most part feel superior. This too is unhelpful because it leads to arrogance and condescension. We look down our noses at others with an air of "I'm better than you!" This leads us to think we don't truly need a Savior, maybe just a little help occasionally.

Jesus taught in this chapter that the more we realize our sin, the more we can realize his grace and love in forgiving our sin. The woman who had a reputation as a scandalous sinner was overwhelmed by Christ's compassion towards her and she showed it with her actions. The smug, self-righteous Pharisee was unaware of his sin. Therefore, he was unaware of his need for a Savior. He had some interest in Christ, but not a desperate love for and appreciation of Christ.

Which character in the story do you identify with most? Do you tend to think of yourself as pretty put together? You know that you aren't perfect, but in comparison with others you must admit that you are doing well and standing tall above the crowd. If you honestly feel that way, I wonder what your worship is like. I wonder how strong your affections are for Christ. How passionately do you live for him each day?

Or do you identify with the woman more? Are you soaked with guilt and shame? Are you overwhelmed with what you've done? Are you embarrassed of how public your sinful reputation is? There is obviously a lot of pain that comes with such a situation. But there is also much hope. Those who are clear about their wretchedness before a holy God have a much better opportunity to experience his grace and love in a transformative way, bringing them out of the guilt and shame, just as this woman was changed.

The point is not that if you have lived too clean of a life you need to run out and commit some scandalous sin to better appreciate Christ. The point is that we are all desperate sinners. Some of us look better externally than others, but compared to Christ we are all exceedingly sinful.

Even if we have lived a very upright life externally, look on the inside. How much do you struggle with pride, hate, anger, small white lies? When you are in a situation where you compare yourself to others, what makes you feel good about yourself? Do you boast about your outward morality?

The Pharisee in this story inwardly boasted of his law-keeping. The Pharisees had added to the Mosaic law to make it stricter than it was. Not touching a known sinful woman would have been an addition to the Mosaic law. But this was part of what he boasted about.

One of the right uses of the moral law of God today is to show us our sin at deeper and deeper levels. It is designed to continually make us increasingly aware of the depth of our sin. The goal is not to leave us in our guilt and shame but rather to drive us out of ourselves. The law, when used rightly, drives us away from the impossibility of our own, self-made righteousness to rest more fully in the salvation Christ has purchased for us with his life and death and resurrection.

The next time you are in a situation where you feel insecure and are tempted to boast in your own righteousness try to catch yourself. Try to quit the comparison game forever. Rather than boasting in some morality trait that you excel in, look to Christ with eyes of faith. Look to your Savior. Look to his finished work on your behalf. Look at his perfect righteousness imputed to you!

This look of faith will humble you. It will increase your joy and thankfulness in and unto Christ. It will also make you more kind, gracious, and compassionate to others that may look outwardly more sinful to you. It can also serve to build your confidence in front of others that may seem to have their lives more perfectly crafted than you do.

How was the known scandalous sinner so humble yet so bold? How could she come to a party for the put-together people even though she wasn't invited? How did she have so much confidence to walk in, weep, and wash Jesus's feet in such a lavish display to ruin the whole affair in the eyes of the host?

All her confidence came from Christ. All her hope came from his love. All her boldness came from forgiveness.

She did not walk arrogantly and proudly with her head held high and her eyes defiant. She didn't have a devil-may-care attitude that scorned the Pharisee. She was not some modern-day liberal, thinking, "No one can judge me. I set my own moral standards. I am above traditional values!"

She came in bold yet humble. She came in confident yet crushed. She came in determined yet lowly. She had been broken by grace.

She knew, much more than the Pharisee knew, how wicked she really was. But she was not overwhelmed by such knowledge because she also knew how forgiven she was. She knew how loved she was. She truly knew Jesus, and the Pharisee did not.

Experiencing the gospel is the most powerful reality in the world. Knowing deeply the twin truths that I am a wicked, damnable sinner and yet I'm loved, secured, and forgiven in Christ is life changing. The simultaneous, seemingly opposed truths are transformative when they sink into the basement of our hearts.

Let the moral law of God have its way with you. Let it convict you as a sinner. Left to ourselves we are rotten, exposed, and hopeless. But let the law also direct you outside of yourself. As you despair afresh of ever saving yourself, remember the one true law keeper, the Lord Jesus Christ. Look at him anew by faith. See his smile. Feel his grace. Know his warmth and tender compassion for you.

Be forgiven. Feel refreshed by his grace and love. He fulfilled all the law for his people. He took the curse of the law on the cross for us. He rose again victoriously, never to die again!

If we are in Christ, we have lived with him, died with him, and risen with him. Our "life is hidden with Christ in God" (Col 3:3). Meditate on justification by faith alone, not by our works. But justification is by works. It is by the perfect, cleansing work of Christ.

Think about your adoption. Remember your freedom in Christ. Boast in your security that he has bought so dearly for you. He is my strength, my righteousness, my confidence, my boast, my all! He is my identity. He is my covenant! Rest in the finished work of Christ for you!

Chapter 7

Law as Command, Not Covenant

THIS CHAPTER BRINGS US to the center of the book as well as to the heart of the topic we are addressing. Everything up until now has been foundational. We have been making sure all the mental furniture is in place to understand the main argument of the book. We will begin by examining the book of Galatians more in depth.

Galatians is commonly called the Magna Carta of Christian liberty. If you struggle with legalism, it is a great place to start your study to better understand the Christian gospel. Paul spends the first four and a half of the six chapters building a case from his own testimony as well as the Old Testament that no one is saved by works. Christians are free from the law as a means to build a relationship with God. They are free from the law as a covenant. They are free from the covenant of works. They are free from the Mosaic covenant. They are free from having to obey the ceremonial and civic laws of Moses.

He is very passionate and emphatic about the freedom we have in Christ. He is writing to refute the false teaching of the Judaizers that believed that gentiles who placed their faith in Christ must be circumcised as the Mosaic law taught. He is so angry at their teaching he wishes they would emasculate themselves (Gal 5:12).

But in the very next verse the tenor and goal of his argument shifts. That is what we will examine in this chapter. Paul has essentially spent four and a half chapters saying, "Don't fall into the ditch of legalism. Don't try and secure your salvation through your own law-keeping." Now he switches and says, "But neither fall into the ditch of licentiousness and libertinism."

Freedom Vs. License

Paul reminds the believers in Gal 5:13 that they have been called to freedom. We are free in Christ from having to work to earn our salvation. John Calvin sums up this reality, teaching that Christ "delivers us from the severity of the law so that he does not deal with us according to its covenant, nor does he bind our consciences under its condemnation."[1] But Paul warns that we should not turn our freedom into an opportunity to sin.

Christians have been making this sinful mistake since the very beginning of the church. When we hear that we are free in Christ, we can think that means we are free to do whatever we want to, including sin. But nothing could be further from the truth. Before we are Christians, we were literally slaves to sin. We had to sin, as Rom 6:19–20 teaches. Freedom in Christ means that we are free to be who we were originally made and intended to be. We are free to know God, love God, and obey God. We are free to live up to all our righteous potential in Christ, not to keep wallowing in our sins.

Imagine a fish that feels "confined" by being stuck in water all day. It longs to be freed from these boundaries enforced upon it by its Creator, so it leaps to "freedom" on the banks of the river. As it lays in the sand and the sun, it will slowly die. Fish were created to survive and thrive in water. It cannot live outside of water. Likewise, human beings are created to survive and thrive in obedience to their Creator. Live outside of obedience long enough and you will die. "There is a way which seems right to a man, / But its end is the way of death" (Prov 14:12).

Paul is wise enough to know there is a ditch of disobedience on either side of gospel living. There is the ditch of legalism where we overvalue that law, even seeing it as a way that we can be justified before God through our own obedience. But likewise, on the other side of the road is the ditch of licentiousness or of being a libertine, whereby we think that God doesn't care about our sin at all because Jesus has paid our debt in full, and we are saved by grace. Neither error is true! And we must avoid both.

The ditch of license undervalues the moral law of God in the Christian life. Legalism and license can both be deadly to the Christian life. Both can ruin my walk with God.

So, if I have freedom in Christ, how am I supposed to use it? I should seek to love God's people and serve them. The Puritan author Samuel Bolton teaches, "He that thinks not service to be his freedom thinks not sin to be his bondage, and therefore he is in bondage. . . . Now we are drawn to

1. Bray, *Galatians*, 199.

service, not with cords of fear, but with the bands of love; not by compulsions of conscience, but with the desires of nature (2 Peter 1.4) . . . our love to God is the source of all our obedience to Him."[2]

Christian freedom is an attitude and perspective that enjoys obeying Christ. There is a true desire to obey Christ, however imperfect it may be. I am not obeying merely out of compulsion or because I am trying to earn anything. I am seeking to obey because I love the Savior who died for me.

Paul makes clear in Gal 5:14 that he wants Christians to seek to fulfill the moral law. He summarizes it in the second great commandment, "You shall love your neighbor as yourself" (Gal 5:14b). He does not mean that Christians should be able to fully and perfectly fulfill the law. We cannot. And yet we are to endeavor to obey Christ with as much sincerity and genuine love as we can.

Christ fulfilled the law perfectly to save us. We now fulfill the law imperfectly, as growing children, to please and honor him. "The law cannot touch us, because the penalty of sin is paid," writes John Stott.[3] "We are set free from the law as a way of acceptance, but obliged to keep it as a way of holiness. It is as a ground of justification that the law no longer binds us (for our acceptance we are 'not under law but under grace'). But as a standard of conduct the law is still binding, and we seek to fulfil it, as we walk according to the Spirit."[4] I don't literally, exactly, or fully fulfill the law of God today. But, as a new creation, by God's enabling grace, I do begin to take real baby steps in slowly but surely maturing and keeping the moral law increasingly as I grow. Romans 8:4 speaks to this reality as well.

"The law sends us to the Gospel that we may be justified; and the Gospel sends us to the law again to inquire what is our duty as those who are justified . . . certainly are we much more to learn from the law, which is the image of God in man and the will of God."[5] When a non-Christian confronts the moral law of God they are condemned. They are damned. There is no hope in themselves for salvation. They have broken God's law and can never make amends or repair themselves. Their only hope is to flee to Christ, risen from the dead, as their Savior in the gospel. He perfectly fulfilled the law's demands for them in his life and death. By faith alone in Christ alone a sinner can be saved.

2. Bolton, *True Bounds*, 48–49.

3. Stott, *Men Made New*, 47.

4. Stott, *Men Made New*, 82–83.

5. Bolton, *True Bounds*, 71.

But once one is in Christ, the gospel message sends us back to the moral law not to be condemned but to be counseled, commanded, and instructed. The moral law does tell us how to live practically in this world in such a way as to honor and please Christ. The Scots Confession teaches, "For as God the Father beholds us in the body of his Son Christ Jesus, he accepts our imperfect obedience as if it were perfect, and covers our works, which are defiled with many stains, with the righteousness of his Son. We do not mean that we are so set at liberty that we owe no obedience to the Law."[6]

The Westminster Confession of Faith 18.7 states of the law, "As a rule of life it informs them of God's will and their duty, and directs and binds them to live accordingly." WCF 16.6 says, "Since the persons of believers are accepted through Christ, their good works also are accepted in him. It is not that they are in this life completely without blame and beyond reproof in God's sight, but that God, looking on them in his Son, is pleased to accept and reward that which is sincerely done, although accompanied by many weaknesses and imperfections."

Genuine Christians continue to struggle with sin. But we have been forgiven, covered, and accepted. Further, we have been adopted into God's own family. He is patient and kind. He knows how frail, weak, fragile, and immature we are. Just as a good parent takes delight in a child's first few faltering steps, even though the child might tumble and waddle like a drunken sailor, so God the Father takes great delight at our sincere and genuine attempts at obedience, no matter how weak and faulty they may be.

Christians have been set free from the condemnation of the law. We have been set free to obey God the Father in grace as redeemed children. We have not been set free to sin. We have not been given a license to sin with impunity so that more grace might come, as Paul clearly states in Rom 6:1.

Spirit Vs. Flesh

In Gal 5:16 Paul continues his argument. He instructs the people to live by the Spirit so that they will not obey the desires of the flesh. Paul commands them to "walk by the Spirit," which means that Christians should be empowered by and guided by the Holy Spirit. The Holy Spirit lives in Christians and helps them understand what it means to obey God. The

6. Presbyterian Church (U.S.A.), *Constitution*, 3.15.

Holy Spirit also gives us the power we need to carry out God's commands. Left to our own strength we would never be able to obey God in any respect or degree. We are fully dependent on the Holy Spirit to enable us to obey.

Galatians 5:16 is also a promise. If believers will seek to "walk by the Spirit," they will "not carry out the desire of the flesh." Typically, when Paul uses the phrase "flesh" he is not referring to our skin or our humanity. Rather, he is referring to indwelling sin. John Murray defines "flesh" in Pauline theology as "human nature as controlled and directed by sin."[7]

Christians have the Holy Spirit living inside of them, seeking to empower and guide them. But Christians are not yet perfected and glorified. Sin still lives in us. Sin has been kicked off the throne of our heart. It no longer has ruling authority in our lives. It is no longer the slave master forcing us to obey its will. Now, sin is more like a rebel force fighting for a lost cause. Sin will never totally rule in a Christian's life again. But sin is our sworn enemy, bound and determined to do as much damage in our lives as it possibly can.

Paul is not saying that Christians will never sin again if they just obey the Holy Spirit. Rather, he is saying sin will not reign in us. Slowly but surely sin is dying out inside of us. It is losing its power and grip. To the degree we seek to follow the Holy Spirit's guidance in our lives, sin will lose its influence over us. The Bible speaks of the Holy Spirit's guidance primarily as leading us to Christlikeness. John Calvin is helpful: "The spiritual person is not free from the lusts of the flesh but he does not let them control him, which is what gratifying their desires amounts to."[8] Again he comments, "The sons of God, so long as they groan under the burden of the flesh, are liable to commit sin, they are not its subjects or slaves, but make habitual opposition to its power. The spiritual man may be frequently assaulted by the lusts of the flesh, but he does not *fulfil* them,—he does not permit them to reign over him."[9]

When the Bible talks about being led by the Holy Spirit it primarily means that we are led to a holy life. We are led to kill sin and say no to sinful desires. We are led to obey God's word by his power in our lives.

I am not strong enough to beat back sin in my life in my own strength. It will take supernatural power to make real progress. The Holy Spirit is the one who brings that resurrection power to bear in my life

7. Murray, *Epistle to the Romans*, 244.

8. Bray, *Galatians,* 189.

9. Calvin, *Commentaries on the Epistles*, 162.

At this point we may understandably ask, "How does this happen? How does the Holy Spirit work in my life? How am I progressively freed from sin's power and influence? How can I grow in holiness and practical obedience?"

So much of this is about knowing and obeying God's written word. Paul wrote two letters at almost the exact same time, from the same location, to two churches in a similar area. The letters—to the Ephesians and to the Colossians—were likely carried to these churches by the same courier. When you read these two letters side by side you can see similar themes, patterns, and phrases. You can tell that Paul was delivering very similar material to both churches, though at times he uses slightly different words, etc.

Ephesians 5:18–20 and Col 3:16 are very similar and speak to the concept of being filled with, empowered by, and led by the Holy Spirit. Ephesians 5:18b–20 says, "Be filled with the Spirit, speaking to one another in psalms and hymns and spiritual songs, singing and making melody with your heart to the Lord; always giving thanks for all things in the name of the Lord Jesus Christ to God, even the Father." Colossians 3:16–17 says, "Let the word of Christ richly dwell within you, with all wisdom teaching and admonishing one another with psalms and hymns and spiritual songs, singing with thankfulness in your hearts to God. And whatever you do in word or deed, do all in the name of the Lord Jesus, giving thanks through Him to God the Father."

You can see that these passages are very similar. They also come in a very similar place in each epistle, right before Paul's teaching on marriage and parenting, etc. What is the one clearest difference between the two? In Ephesians we are commanded to "be filled with the Spirit." In Colossians we are commanded to "let the word of Christ richly dwell within you." The most practical way to be filled with and guided by the Holy Spirit is to be filled with and guided by God's written word.

An illustration may help. Imagine you are single and traveling in Italy. You meet someone of the opposite sex who is a strong Christian, beautiful, smart, funny, rich, and single, and you both fall in love with one another. There's just one small problem. You don't speak a lick of Italian and this Italian you love doesn't speak a lick of English. What's the first thing you should do?

I gave this illustration in a college Sunday school class once and asked the class the same question. A fraternity guy from the University of Alabama sitting in the front row answered loudly, "Teach her to speak American!" I knew the guy and responded, "That's why you're still single, buddy."

The right answer if you are truly in love with this person is to learn to speak Italian as quickly as possible so you can communicate with the one you love. As Christians we must learn to speak the language of the Holy Spirit. The Bible is the Holy Spirit's language.

Now, God can speak to us however he chooses to. He can speak through creation and may make a deep impression on your soul through seeing a rainbow or something like that. There's a story in the book of Numbers where God speaks to a prophet through a donkey. The prophet listens to God speaking to him through the donkey. But if you read that story and go buy a donkey in hopes that God will speak to you through your donkey, I think you will be sadly disappointed.

God can speak to us however and whenever he wants to, but he has clearly promised to speak to us through his word. "All Scripture is inspired by God and profitable for teaching, for reproof, for correction, for training in righteousness; that the man of God may be adequate, equipped for every good work" (2 Tim 3:16–17). All the essentials we need to walk with God are given to us in his word. It is sufficient. There is no other authoritative word for our spiritual lives. All obedience starts with faith, and faith grows by hearing God's word (Rom 10:17 and 14:23; Heb 11:6).

Martin Luther is helpful on this topic. "I have suffered many and various passions, and the same also very vehement and great. But as soon as I have laid hold of any place of Scripture, and stayed myself upon it as my chief anchor-hold, immediately temptations vanished away; without the Word it would have been impossible to overcome them."[10] When we face temptations to sin the best thing we can do is think on God's word. Think on commands and promises that point us in the direction of holiness and obedience. As we persevere in meditating on his word, God will provide the power we need to say no to temptation! Here is a wonderfully helpful promise to meditate on the next time you are tempted. "No temptation has overtaken you but such as is common to man; and God is faithful, who will not allow you to be tempted beyond what you are able, but with the temptation will provide the way of escape also, that you may be able to endure it" (1 Cor 10:13).

The Christian life will not be easy. It is literally a battle between indwelling sin and the Holy Spirit that live inside of you (Gal 5:17). Paul

10. Luther, *Commentary on Galatians*, 369.

speaks of this battle at length in Rom 7:14–25. "For that which I am doing, I do not understand; for I am not practicing what I would like to do, but I am doing the very thing I hate. . . . For the good that I wish, I do not do; but I practice the very evil that I do not wish. But if I am doing the very thing I do not wish, I am no longer the one doing it, but sin which dwells in me. I find then the principle that evil is present in me, the one who wishes to do good" (Rom 7:15, 19–21).

Can you identify with Paul in this battle? Paul was not talking about dealing with outward, scandalous sins such as persecuting and murdering Christians. He is talking about inward sins, such as coveting, that are so hard to put fully to death (Rom 7:7–8). Luther said, "The more godly a man is, the more does he feel the battle."[11] Tim Keller taught,

> Even when we know and see ourselves making progress against many bad habits and attitudes, we will grow more aware of the rebellious and selfish roots that are still within us. The holier we are, the more we cry, "What a wretch I am! Who will deliver me from this sin within!" . . . Just as a wounded bear is more dangerous than a healthy and happy bear, our sinful natures might become more stirred up and active because the new birth has mortally wounded it.[12]

Sin is losing in the believer's life. But sin and Satan will do all they can to make his life a miserable fight. We should not expect a sweet, easy journey to heaven. Matthew Poole is very helpful on this passage and Paul's ongoing struggle with sin as well:

> He was not sin's servant or slave; but many times he was sin's captive against his will. . . . Against his will and consent, he was still subject to the violent lusts and assaults of sin, and not able wholly to free himself: though he always made stout resistance, yet many times he was overcome. . . . He doth not speak here so much of outward actions, as of inward motions and affections: he doth not speak of gross sins, as drunkenness, uncleanness, &c., but of such infirmities as flow from the polluted nature, and from which we can never be thoroughly cleansed in this life. . . . The meaning is not that he never did the good he desired; but it often so fell out, he began many good things, but he could not go thorough-stitch with them.[13]

11. Luther, *Commentary on Galatians*, 365.

12. Keller, *Romans*, 103.

13. Poole, *Matthew Poole's Commentary*, 500–501.

Now imagine a legalist reading Gal 5. As they come to Gal 5:17, they might say, "Amen, Paul. You must fight to fulfill the law!" But Paul is careful to avoid the ditch of license as well as legalism. Galatians 5:18 says, "But if you are led by the Spirit, you are not under the Law." What in the world does this mean? It means that Christians are not under the law as a covenant to be saved. It means we are not under the covenant of works. We are not under the law's curses or condemnation, but we are under its commands, counsels, and corrections.

The moral law of God is like a fire. When a fire is in its proper place it is a blessing. It brings warmth, light, beauty, and heat. Fire in the stove can cook food and keep someone alive. Fire in the fireplace can bring comfort to the cold. But if fire gets out and consumes your house, it can kill you.

In a very similar way, the moral law of God in your heart to guide you into obedience is a wonderful thing. For a Christian who is forgiven and wants to please God, his law brings great insight into how to honor Christ in all we do. But to a non-Christian under the law of God, it is terrible thing that condemns one in sin to damnation. "Obedience to the moral law . . . need not necessarily lead to . . . 'legal obedience'; there is a free and evangelical obedience. An unbalanced emphasis on grace has led men to neglect certain of the law's various functions."[14]

I heard an illustration about the law that is helpful. Before someone is in Christ, the moral law of God is like a stick to beat us and punish us for our sin. It exposes our sin and condemns us, rightfully so. But once we have trusted in Christ, Christ hands us this same stick. Now the law is no longer used to beat us. Rather it has become a walking stick to help us along our path.

When the moral law comes to us from the hand of Christ rather than from Moses, it brings rest. Christ said, "Take My yoke upon you, and learn from Me . . . and you shall find rest for your souls. For My yoke is easy, and My load is light" (Matt 11:29–30). When we seek to submit to Christ as our Lord, Master, *and Savior* and thus obey his law and word, we are like a fish returning to the water. It brings life and rest. It is what we were created to do. "His commandments are not burdensome" (1 John 5:3b). To the degree that we are walking by the Spirit, obedience will seem more and more like the right thing, the natural thing. But it will never be full in this life. Indwelling sin will continue to raise its nasty head and fight us every step of the way.

14. Bolton, *True Bounds*, 10.

Paul gets very specific in describing sin in Gal 5:19–21. He breaks it down into four different categories: sexual, witchcraft, relational, and partying. We might ask, can a Christian do one of these sins one time and still be a true Christian? Yes, if someone is truly in Christ, they can never lose their salvation. Paul says clearly, "Those who practice such things will not inherit the kingdom of God" (Gal 5:21b). The key word is practice. The pattern of a true Christian's life will be more and more towards godliness over the long haul. If someone was to watch your life for a decade and they saw a pattern of sexual sin, witchcraft, hate for other people, and drunkenness, it would be fair to draw the conclusion that you are not a genuine believer, regardless of what you may say with your mouth about Christ.

The trend of your life speaks to sin continuing to be on the throne of your life. Frank Barker, the founding pastor of Briarwood Presbyterian Church in Birmingham, used to say, "It's not about the perfection of your life. It is about the direction of your life. Faith that fizzles before the finish was false from the first."[15] For genuine believers, slowly but surely, there will be a putting off of sin, and a putting on of righteousness. Remaining sin in a Christian's life is real but not reigning.[16]

But just because we have these great and mighty promises that sin will not reign in us, we cannot rest in a passive way and assume indwelling sin will just lay down and quit. When it seems sin is leaving us alone, beware. Sin will lull us into its confidence. It will convince us it is dead by lying dormant awhile. Then, when we let our guard down, it will spring into action when we least suspect it. We must already be ready, willing, and able to catch and kill sin when it first makes itself known. Killing sin "is the deliberate rejection of any sinful thought, suggestion, desire, aspiration, deed, circumstance or provocation at the moment we become conscious of its existence. It is the consistent endeavor to do all in our powers to weaken the grip which sin in general, and its manifestations in our lives in particular, has."[17] Imagine someone was trying to stab you with a knife. How would you respond? You would watch their attacks carefully. You would respond to each of their thrusts with a motion of defense. You would match each stab with a feint. You would be hyperaware and vigilant, and so we should be with indwelling sin.

15. In personal conversation with the author.

16. Ferguson, *Christian Life*, 146.

17. Ferguson, *Christian Life*, 150.

John Owen, one of the greatest theologians of all time, said, "Make it your daily occupation. Do not cease a day from this work. Be killing sin or it will kill you." He goes further, "We are to renew our inward man 'day by day' . . . in spite of the mortification exhibited in the cross of Christ for each and every sin, we must apply its efficacy by our daily mortification of the flesh."[18] Mortification means to kill. Jesus's death on the cross brings the decisive power to kill the authority of sin in our lives. But we must appropriate that power. The Christian must work daily, in conjunction with and dependence on the Holy Spirit, to practically bring the power of Christ to bear in our lives. This will literally be a lifelong process. Christ has struck the death blow to indwelling sin for us. But it dies a slow death. We are to use his resurrection, blood-bought power to fully and finally put sin to death practically in our lives.

Poole teaches, "Fall into [sin] they may, but live in it they cannot. It is not falling into the water that drowns a man, but it is his lying in it; so it is not falling into sin that damns a man, but it is his living in it."[19] Falling into water doesn't kill someone. Drowning in water does. Falling into sin doesn't condemn the Christian, but drowning in sin proves one was never a true Christian in the first place. Christians will continue to be tempted by and struggle with sin. But, by God's grace, we must do all we can to put sin to death in our lives.

But simply putting sin to death is not enough to make progress in the Christian life. We must put off the old life but also put on the new. In Gal 5:22–23 Paul lists the fruit of the Holy Spirit. Basically, he tells us there will be several positive character traits that begin to blossom in our lives as we resist sin and follow the lead of the Holy Spirit. The Holy Spirit leads his people to be practically holy in day-to-day life.

Galatians 5:24 says, "Now those who belong to Christ Jesus have crucified the flesh with its passion and desires." If someone has genuinely come to Christ there has been a decisive, once-and-for-all break with the past sinful life. It is very much like marriage.

When a man walks down the aisle and vows to be faithful to his wife, he is saying no, once and for all, to every other woman at that moment. Ideally this is the beginning of a lifetime of faithful marriage. But even in the best marriages, there will be sin and struggles. A married man may never sleep with anyone other than his wife. But he might have many lustful

18. Owen, *Sin and Temptation*, 160–61.

19. Poole, *Matthew Poole's Commentary*, 496.

thoughts. It will be a battle to be faithful. It will not always come naturally or easily.

In a similar way, when we come to Christ, we are marrying him spiritually. We are committing to him. There is a once-and-for-all lifetime commitment to love, trust, and obey Christ in all we say, think, feel, desire, and do. But then each day we must wake up and practically fight sin, put it to death, and pursue practical holiness.

How do we practically do this sanctifying work of putting sin to death? Primarily we use the word of God on ourselves. We think about it and then, by grace, seek to obey and apply it. Luther again is helpful: "The nails are the word of God that penetrate by the impulse of God's grace and prevent the flesh from following its own desires."[20] Luther is commenting on Gal 5:24 and telling us that our practical experience of crucifying sin in our lives will come through the power of God's written word, believed and applied in our lives.

Paul summarizes this argument, saying, "If we live by the Spirit, let us also walk by the Spirit" (Gal 5:25). If we have been given new life in Christ by the Holy Spirit, then let us daily live by the Holy Spirit's power and guidance. If Christ chose to give us the gift of salvation and the Holy Spirit, we should follow the Holy Spirit in our daily lives we now live.

Compassion and Comparison

Paul has made his argument against licentious living in Gal 5:13–25. In verse 26 he begins to apply these principles to the church at Galatia in a very specific way. The reality is all Christians will at times struggle with versions of legalism and with licentiousness.

When you have any type of works-based religious culture this will never lead you toward loving others. It will lead in the opposite direction. It will lead you towards an evil comparison game. You may often act loving on the outside, but internally you will not be genuinely loving others as you should.

Think about it. If my whole sense of self-worth and spiritual identity is built on and wrapped up in how well I'm performing spiritually, then I will always be scanning the horizon for a sense of how well I'm doing. The easiest way to evaluate myself will be in comparison to others.

20. Bray, *Galatians,* 200.

I will either see others that seem much better than I am and thus feel like a loser. Or I will see others struggling more than I am, at least outwardly so, and feel superior. Either attitude will not lead to actively loving them. Rather I am using them in my own spiritual quest for self-worth. I may look down on them in arrogance and condescension. Or I may look up to them in envy and jealousy. But to simply love them as a brother or sister in Christ will be nearly impossible. Paul knows this. Paul lived this way before he was a believer.

Paul confronts these sinful attitudes head-on in Gal 5:26, commanding us not to envy one another, nor to be boastful and challenging. If I think I'm better than others I will boast and brag. I will be arrogant and brash. If I'm not sure how I'm doing in the comparison game, I may be challenging, pushing others' buttons, trying to get a rise out of them and discover their weaknesses. If I'm sure I'm doing worse than others, I'll be filled with envy for what others have and how much better they are doing than I am. I'll weep when others succeed and rejoice when they fail.

Legalists are hard on all people—themselves and others. It's legalistic to play the comparison game at all in our ultimate evaluation of ourselves and others. But then we often respond in outwardly licentious ways when we may let fly critical or envious looks, words, or worse.

Paul shows us a better way in Gal 6:1. The way of love is to help others. If we see them stuck in a pattern of sin, we should not look down on them in disdain. Nor should we rejoice that now we are winning the comparison game. Rather, we should seek to help them in love. We should be moved with bold compassion to help them. We should take the first step towards them and not wait for them to ask for help.

There is boldness and confidence in Christ because of what he is doing in me. But there is also humility because of remaining, indwelling sin. I approach others to help in a spirit of caution and meekness, knowing that I may fall into the same sin they are stuck in.

"Bear one another's burdens and thus fulfill the law of Christ" (Gal 6:2). When I, in a spirit of love, genuinely try to help a brother or sister in Christ fight sin and make progress, I am fulfilling the law of Christ. What is the law of Christ? It is the moral law of God, coming to me from Christ in the covenant of grace and not from Moses in the covenant of works. It is not a covenant for me to keep for salvation. It is a command to keep inside the covenant of grace to please and honor Christ.

Some Christians would teach that the Old Testament moral law has no more relevance for Christians today. They are wrong. The law of Christ is the same moral law from the Old Testament. Notice that when New Testament authors speak of the law of love, they explicitly cite passages from the Ten Commandments as the abiding rule for Christians, as in Rom 13:8–10 and Jas 2:8–11. If some pagan gentile came to faith and was learning of the law of Christ, they might ask, "How do I know how to love my neighbor well practically?" Paul or James could simply reply with the Ten Commandments. "Don't kill your neighbor, don't sleep with his wife, don't steal from him, don't lie to him. That's how you practically love your neighbor and fulfill the law of Christ."

When I live and love like this, I am fulfilling the law of Christ. I am not fulfilling it sinlessly but with real sincerity, and thus Christ is pleased. Love God and love your neighbor. Obey the Ten Commandments. Love and obey not to secure your salvation. You already have that secured in Christ. Love and obey to please and honor your Savior.

Sibbes is helpful again:

> What is the gospel itself but a merciful moderation, in which Christ's obedience is esteemed ours, and our sins laid upon him, wherein God, from being a judge, becomes our Father, pardoning our sins and accepting our obedience, though feeble and blemished? . . . In the covenant of works, this [law] must be fulfilled absolutely, but under that covenant of grace it must have an evangelical mitigation. A sincere endeavor proportionable to grace received is accepted. . . . Under this gracious covenant, sincerity is perfection.[21]

In Christ, I do my best by grace to love God and neighbor, and God is truly pleased with me. What freedom! What joy! What grace!

Bolton speaks in a similarly powerful and freeing way:

> The Gospel admits repentance but the law will not own it. . . . Though there may be failing action, yet where there is truth of affection, God can own it. In the Gospel God accepts affections for actions, endeavours for performance, desire for ability. A Christian is made up of desires, of mournings, thirstings and bewailings: O that my ways were directed! O miserable man that I am! Here is Gospel perfection.[22]

21. Sibbes, *Bruised*, 36–37.

22. Bolton, *True Bounds*, 42.

Application

We will all struggle at times with legalism and licentiousness. But most of us tend to struggle with one more than the other. It is important and helpful to know yourself well. Knowing your typical struggle will help you in your fight against indwelling sin.

One way to understand yourself better is to ask yourself who you struggle to love the most. In what situations do you have the hardest time loving people? Do you tend to struggle more with envying those that you think are ahead of you? Or do you struggle more with looking down on those seemingly behind you in the Christian race?

And when you struggle in the comparison game, how does that struggle manifest itself in your life? Do you have arrogant and biting words of criticism? Do you give yourself over to endless envious thoughts? Or do you simply ignore those who struggle and are in need of your help? The better you know yourself, the better you can begin and progress in putting your sin to death with the help of God's Spirit and word.

Conclusion

Antinomianism is a belief that Christians are free from any obligation whatsoever to obey God's moral law. Sinclair Ferguson teaches that

> legalism and antinomianism are, in fact, nonidentical twins that emerge from the same womb. Eve's rejection of God's law (antinomianism) was in fact the fruit of her distorted view of God (legalism). . . . Once the "lie about God" was injected into the human genome, so to speak, it took up permanent lodging deep in the human psyche. It is the default position of the natural man. . . . How do I think about God and what instincts and dispositions and affections toward him does this evoke in me? At that level legalism and antinomianism share a common root that has invaded not only mind but heart, affections, and will—how we feel toward God as well as the doctrine of God we profess. . . . Legalism is also related to the heart and the affections—how we feel about God. We do not relate to God in an affection- and emotion-free context . . . but as whole persons—mind, will, dispositions, motivations, and affections in varying degrees of integrity or disintegration. Within this matrix legalism at root is the manifestation of a restricted heart disposition toward God, viewing him through a lens

> of negative law that obscures the broader context of the Father's character of holy love.[23]

This is why legalism and antinomianism, or lawlessness, can be operating simultaneously in one person's heart at the same time in different ways. They share the same starting point: a distrust of God's good character.

The legalist thinks and feels that God isn't good, so I must earn his love through good works. The lawless person thinks and feels that God isn't good, so I can't trust him to give me good gifts. So, I must break his law to get the joy and pleasure in life I want and need. Whether you struggle more with legalism or lawlessness, the root is the same. And thus, the glorious answer is the same.

Look to Christ. Look at the cross. Stare and see afresh how Christ has loved you. Be convinced again in the basement of your heart how good and wonderful he is!

Who are you struggling to love the most right now in your life? Where are you the most sick and tired of bearing someone else's burden because they are so weak, selfish, sinful, or stupid? Remember how Christ has loved you. "He left his Father's throne above, / So free, so infinite his grace . . . / And bled for Adam's helpless race!"[24] He made the first move to come to us and lift the heavy burden of sin from our lives. He put it on his own back and went to the cross for us. He took the curse of the law and the wrath of God that all his people deserved.

With his life, death, and resurrection he extinguished once and for all the wrath of God for his people. He has dealt with our ultimate burden for us, before we were born. Let your heart start to sing. Then think again of the person you struggle to love. Maybe they even feel like an enemy at times. Maybe they are your nemesis or the thorn in your side. By the grace of Christ love them well. Lift burdens off their life as you can because Christ has taken so much off your life that you could not save yourself from.

23. Ferguson, *Whole*, 84.

24. Wesley, "And Can It Be?"

Chapter 8

Right Ways to Use the Law

In this chapter we will examine the right ways for a Christian to use the moral law in his or her life. We all struggle with lawlessness at times. Antinomians (those who don't prioritize the moral law as they should) have two problems. First, they do not value the moral law as they should. "Free from law" is their mantra. Secondly, they do not realize how strong, evil, and deadly indwelling sin is in them, even after their conversion.

Romans 7–8 is the main place Paul deals with both errors the most clearly and thoroughly. Romans 7:7–13 seems to be slightly autobiographical for Paul. But the principles it teaches are true for every person, even going back to Adam to some degree. It shows us how the moral law functions in our lives.

In the book of Romans, Paul has been at pains to show that no one can be saved by works. Salvation by law-keeping is impossible. No one can earn their salvation or justify themselves by strict obedience to God's moral law.

In mounting this attack against the concept of salvation by law, Paul knows that he has been talking very negatively about the law. He realizes that some may come to see the law as something evil to be despised. Now, he sets out to head off and correct that potential mistake in his readers.

In Rom 7:7 he asks the question, "Is the Law sin?" Is God's moral law contained in the Ten Commandments given to Moses bad? He responds in the strongest way possible. "May it never be!" No, never! The law showed me my sin more fully. It rightfully condemned me in my sinfulness. It thus drove me away from my own attempts at self-salvation. It drove me out of myself into the arms of my Savior.

The law shows us how sinful we are. The law exposes self-righteousness as a farce. The law will drive us to Christ.

Everything about the moral law is pure, holy, just, and righteous. Its weakness is that it is powerless to save. We must look to the law and use the law only as God intended, no more, no less.

The law stirs up sin in our lives. It exposes sin in our lives. It can seem to be a bad thing for this reason, but it is a helpful thing.

Imagine if a thief was caught red-handed in their crime and taken to jail. If they sit in jail, angry at the police that they are in jail they miss the point. The cops did nothing wrong. In fact, the police did everything right. They did their job and enforced the law. The thief is the guilty one for choosing to steal. But in his anger and rage he may blame the police officers: "If they hadn't come, I could have gotten away with my crime!" He may feel justified in blaming them, but they only exposed the crime he was already committing.

In a similar way, we can be frustrated at the law sometimes for being too strict or unrealistic. But the law is never a problem. Out sinfulness is. The law is moral, upright, good, and beautiful. Rightly understood, it is the means of our salvation, for by it, the Lord Jesus saved us.

After Rom 7:13 Paul will switch from the past tense to present-tense verbs. He has been discussing the law's role in his conversion. But now he discusses the law in his present life as a Christian, as he writes the letter to the Romans. He is going to illustrate for us the right ways to use the law as a Christian.

In Rom 7:14—8:13 he is doing much of what he did in Gal 5:13–25. He is intentionally combating those who might tend to lean toward antinomianism. He's said so many negative things about the law (as a way of justification) that he realizes he may be pushing some immature Christians to jettison the law from their lives fully. And this was never his intent. He will show us three main ways the law is still used in a Christian's life. It *directs*, it *discloses*, and it *drives*.

Directs

Samuel Bolton teaches, "The law is abrogated in respect of its power to justify or condemn; but it remains full of force to direct us in our lives. It condemns sin in the faithful, though it cannot condemn the faithful for sin."[1] He also says, "The law sends us to the Gospel for our justification; the Gospel sends us to the law to frame our way of life."[2] Brandon Crowe says, "Even though we can't perfectly obey God's law, the law continues to guide us in how we should live. Obedience to God's law is required. And yet obedience is not a burden but the path of blessing."[3] The law does not condemn the believer. The law cannot be perfectly obeyed in this life. Yet, the law is still very useful, important, and necessary to grow and please God in our lives.

In Rom 7:14 Paul says, "The Law is spiritual." This means it shows us what practical obedience God desires from us.[4] One of my sons disobeyed once in an obvious way but feigned ignorance. I asked him to write down what he thought his priorities in life ought to be. The first three he wrote down were: honor God, honor neighbor, honor parents. Where did he get those from? Where did he even get the language of "honor" from? He got it from the law of God, from the Bible, and specifically from the Ten Commandments.

Partially, this law is written on every human's heart. But my son has grown up in the church and an imperfect Christian family trying to raise him in the nurture and admonition of the Lord. He knows the Ten Commandments. He knows Jesus's summary of the law as loving God and loving neighbor. The law of God is written on every human heart. But it is unclear to some degree because of indwelling sin. Thus, the law is not totally intuitive to us. We need the written word of God to fully reveal to us God's law.

Christians still need this. Christians need the Bible speaking to us with force and clarity and reminding us of God's eternal truth. We need the Bible to tell us to rest one day in seven. Remember the Sabbath day to keep it holy.

Imagine someone grew up in a godless nation and country but met a missionary and came to Christ. This person is a genuine convert. But they are only acquainted with Rom 3 as far as the Bible is concerned. That was the chapter the missionary used to explain the gospel. If this is the only special revelation they have been exposed to, will they be able to discern on their own that one of God's Ten Commandments is to rest from their normal labors one day out of every seven? No, they will not. They might

1. Bolton, *True Bounds*, 58.
2. Bolton, *True Bounds*, 11.
3. Crowe, *Path*, 2.
4. Stott, *Men*, 73.

discern that rest is a good thing in general. But to discern a pattern of one day of rest out of seven takes God's written word. Christians need God's written word and written law to clearly show them all the good God requires from them as his people. God's written law directs us to the truth of who God is and what he wants from us.

Think about 2 Cor 9:6–7, which commands Christians to give their money to the church and or to the poor. It also commands us to do it with a cheerful heart, not reluctantly or under compulsion. Would every Christian fully understand this instinctively without written clarity? I dare say that many Christians tend to "forget" this truth, even though it has been clearly written for us. We need God's moral law to guide, confront, remind, and exhort us. This is one reason that the apostle tells Timothy, his protégé, to constantly be teaching God's word to God's people (1 Tim 3:16—4:5).

Antinomians, those who disregard God's moral law in their lives, either forget or downplay the reality and the power of indwelling sin in believers' lives. Yes, sin has been dethroned. It no longer has ruling power and authority in our lives. It does still have much power to frustrate my Christian walk and do damage to my spiritual growth.

There are many Christians who will argue about exactly who or what type of person Paul is describing in the second half of Rom 7. Some will say he describes a non-Christian; others will say it is an immature Christian or a legalistic Christian. Some may say that he is describing an Old Testament believer before the new giving of the Holy Spirit.

Most of the best commentators, including Augustine, Luther, Calvin, and more would say that Paul is describing a mature believer. He is describing a mature believer who still struggles with sinful temptations. He describes his own experience as a believer of over twenty years who is an apostle called upon to write much of the New Testament.[5]

Why does sin still seem so powerful in his life and in ours? Because sin in the Christian's life has been dealt the death blow, but it is not dead yet. It is like a wounded animal in its death throes. Sin, personified in us, is mad at God and trying to do all the damage it can before it finally expires.

Antinomians love to say things like, "Now I'm so free in Christ and empowered by grace, all I need to do is think about Jesus and the cross and all will be well in my life." The problem is that isn't true. It is not what the Bible teaches. If this were true, why would the Bible spend so much time

5. For details on this debate see Calvin, *Commentaries*, 259–61.

in the New Testament epistles instructing Christians very specifically how to obey Christ?

If you were going to honestly describe the battle in your own life between sin and righteousness, how would you describe it? Would it not sound like Rom 7:14–25? And remember, don't think so much of outward scandalous sins as much as the inward, hidden sins of the heart. Think about sinful anger, lust, greed, envy, jealousy, and worry. How easy are these sins to finally and fully put to death?

Remember that the struggle Paul describes is in the context of the command "You shall not covet" (Rom 7:7). He is not saying that he still wrestles with his worst, pre-Christian sins. He does not say that occasionally, he sneaks out of his house and goes and tortures and imprisons some Christians as he did before the Damascus Road experience. He is a genuinely, radically changed man. But he is not a sinlessly perfect man.

There are some sins that many Christians seem to make instantaneous progress against in the Christian life, such as drunkenness. But then there are smaller, sneakier sins that seem to root themselves deeply in the hearts of the strongest Christians, like pride and sinful comparison.

My old pastor, Harry Reeder, used to say that God would tend to microwave one or two sins out of a believer's life early in conversion to convince them their conversion was real. But then many of the other sins were put into the Crock-Pot of sanctification. It may literally take a lifetime to see real progress against some of the sins in our lives.

Think of the sin of worry. Virtually no one plans to worry. We do not intentionally set aside time to worry. Worry seems more like the flu. It sneaks up on us. It abducts us. It overtakes us seemingly out of nowhere. One moment, we are at peace. The next we are worrying and we aren't even exactly sure when or how it started.

I am not saying we are helpless victims before our sins. We are not. We have a part to play in capturing and killing remaining sin in our lives. And to fight this battle we need God's law to clearly point out all the sin in our lives so that we can appropriately kill it.

The law gives me great clarity about what is sin and what is righteousness. The Bible speaks of a proper type of concern for people that is not sinful worry. But the Bible also describes a type of concern that is sinful and anxious because it does not trust God's provision. How can I know the difference between proper concern and sinful concern? I must have the moral law of God directing my mind and directing my fight against sin.

God's law's intention in my life is very helpful. But the law does not have the power to enable me to kill sin. If it is just me and the law fighting sin, I will fail eventually. But I should never use God's saving grace as an excuse for sin. Bolton teaches, "To make Christian liberty the cloak of sin: that is most damnable."[6]

Discloses

The law not only directs, instructs, and points me in the right direction; it also inspects, exposes, and discloses to me how deep and buried sin is in me. We honestly have no idea how deep the roots of rebellion go in our hearts. The tentacles of inward corruption run to the core. We are not utterly depraved, meaning that we are not as sinful as we potentially could be. But we are still sinful to some degree in all that we do as long as sin remains in us. Even our best deeds need to be cleansed by the blood of Christ.

How many of us have decided at some point something like, "I will cut all sweet foods out for the next month!" Sounds easy enough. We are mature Christians bearing the Holy Spirit fruit of self-control. The first week comes easy and naturally. The second week takes more effort. The third week seems like a real struggle. In the fourth week someone makes our favorite dessert just for us and we feel it would be mean to say no. We give in so our friend doesn't feel bad. We see how weak our self-control is. A law commanding us to be self-controlled has exposed how much I lack the discipline I ought to have.

This one example may not connect with you. But my guess is we all have at least one area where we feel like we are often losing the battle of sanctification. We have areas that feel at best like two steps forward, one step back.

As we seek to fight sin, the law is like a shovel that digs deep into our hearts. It exposes us to ourselves. It discloses to us the depths of our remaining sin. The harder we fight against sin the tighter we will realize its grip is. It can feel at times like resisting Chinese handcuffs that tighten as we pull against the restraints.

Ambrose said that "the law is the discoverer, not the begetter of sin."[7] Our sinfulness is not the law's fault. But the law does stir and expose sin in

6. Bolton, *True Bounds*, 20.

7. Quoted in Calvin, *Commentaries on the Epistle*, 252.

our lives. The more we read, study, and seek to apply the law in our lives, at times, it can seem like we get worse before we get better.

Romans 7:17 says, "So now, no longer am I the one doing it, but sin which indwells me." Paul is not trying to shirk all responsibility here for his sinfulness. Rather, he is making the point that he is a new creation in Christ. Sin is no longer his identity. Sin is no longer natural for him. Yet, much of the same old sin remains alive inside him. It still has much influence, power, and sway. It often feels natural for saints although, in reality, it no longer is.

Sin does not have ruling authority in any Christians' lives. But it seems at times to have overwhelming power and influence. It is a lifelong battle to fully and finally put sin to death. And the battle will never be done until we see Christ face-to-face.

Part of the Christian life is to read, study, and meditate on God's word and let it have its own way with us. Let it do heart surgery on us. I have known that I struggled with anger since I was a child. And yet, at times, when I read and meditate on God's slowness to anger, I can be convicted in an even deeper way. My impatience and quickness in anger can look more wretched, evil, and wicked than ever before. The reality is I've made gigantic strides in patience and gentleness by God's grace in the last thirty-plus years. And yet, when I compare myself honestly to God, his character and word, I'm humbled and broken afresh. The law seems to shine a light on the deep, dark, remaining roots of my self-centered sin. Prayerfully read God's word daily, asking the Holy Spirit to shine a loving searchlight deeper into your soul to expose the areas of your remaining sinfulness that may be hidden from the plain light of day.

In Rom 7:18 Paul says, "Nothing good dwells in me . . . for the wishing is present in me, but the doing of the good is not." All true Christians truly desire to obey God's word in their innermost being. But we do not have the power to do it left to ourselves. We have the desire but not the ability. And the law cannot bring the power to be holy. Calvin said, "The law by itself is destructive."[8]

The law can instruct, it can expose, but it cannot change. Christians can know God's word perfectly and yet still sin. Our struggle with sin will be an ongoing reality to the grave. There is so much we know we should do and want to do, yet we still fail to fully obey.

8. Calvin, *Commentaries on the Epistle*, 250.

Sin is deep in our hearts. Sin lurks in every nook and cranny and corner of our hearts. The law comes like a searchlight to expose and help us destroy this remaining iniquity.

Romans 7:21 says, "I find then the principle that evil is present in me, the one who wishes to do good." Sin is like the shadow of a Christian. Even in our best moments of worship and obedience in the light of his presence, sin lurks nearby. It is right behind us. It is never far away even if we do not see it in the moment. We will not fully be removed from sin's presence until we are with God in glory.

Because of this reality, we will live in tension. In the gap between our good, godly desires and our failure to fulfill them lies the key to understanding Rom 7:14–25. Just as he had in Gal 5, Paul tells us in Rom 7:23 that a war rages inside of every Christian. A war raged between Paul's godly desires and the power of indwelling sin to corrupt him. At every turn he is followed, hounded, and checked by sin. And so are we. This battle makes him and us feel like a prisoner trapped inside our own body, full of conflicting desires and actions.

Drives

The law shows us how to live. The law shows us how far we fall short. And then the law drives us out of ourselves to another.

The law, for the Christian, rightly applied, should continually drive us away from our own self-centered efforts and into the arms of Christ. He is the only one powerful enough to fully and finally defeat sin in our lives. John Owen teaches that all false religions are ultimately about trying to kill sin in "self-strength."[9]

We can hear and feel Paul's self-disgust in Rom 7:24. "Wretched man that I am! Who will set me free from the body of this death?" Have you ever felt this way? I know I have. When struggling with the same old sin I will often find myself thinking or saying, "What's wrong with me? I'm tired of myself! I'm sick of myself! Part of me just wants to die and go to heaven and be with Christ and be done with this same old struggle!"

In that moment I am feeling my wretchedness and weakness. I am being confronted with the futility of trying to fight sin in my own strength. It never works. I always fail if left to my own devices. It is debilitating.

9. Quoted in Ferguson, *Christian Life*, 149.

Praise God the chapter does not end there in hopelessness. It continues, "Thanks be to God through Jesus Christ our Lord!" (Rom 7:25). There is power. There is freedom. There is progress. There is victory, by and by!

When you struggle the most with sin and get sick of yourself, you may pray and think, "Why am I this way? What am I to do? Is there no hope or help?!" But then remember Christ! Preach Christ to yourself! Remind yourself of his great goodness and grace, greater than all our sin and guilt.

John Stott teaches that the Christian is always praying this prayer. This is not a onetime cry of desperation where a believer once and for all passes from Rom 7 to Rom 8. Rather, it is the ongoing struggle believers live in.[10] Christians should be fully convinced Christ will win the battle against sin in their lives and yet they must continue to fight the battle as long as they live. Stott reminds us, "The law cannot touch us, because the penalty of sin is paid."[11] Stott also says, "We are set free from the law as a way of acceptance, but obliged to keep it as a way of holiness. It is as a ground of justification that the law no longer binds us (for our acceptance we are 'not under the law but under grace'). But as a standard of conduct the law is still binding, and we seek to fulfill it, as we walk according to the Spirit."[12]

Remember that in the original writing of the Bible there were no chapter or verse divisions. So, we need not stop at the end of Rom 7 with this discussion. We can proceed seamlessly in Paul's thoughts into Rom 8.

Although so much sin still lives in me, I will never be condemned. I am free. I am justified. "There is therefore now no condemnation for those who are in Christ Jesus" (Rom 8:1). What a sweet and powerful reminder that we need often to hear. The law drives us to confront this reminder often. Because without Christ living in us, we would be condemned by his law.

It is especially sweet on the heels of a real battle with sin. When we feel bloodied and weary from pushing back on temptation and not coming away unscathed, it is so needful to know we are secure. We are loved by Christ and secure in him, not because of our merit but because of his.

The Holy Spirit has come into your life and kicked sin off the throne of your life. Further, you are in Christ so you are no longer under the covenant of works. Rather, you are now, by grace, under the covenant of grace.

10. Stott, *Men*, 77–78.

11. Stott, *Men*, 47.

12. Stott, *Men*, 82–83.

The law could not save us. The law could not free us. The law could not justify us. But Christ could. Christ did. Christ lived under the law sinlessly for us. Then he died in our place, taking our wrath and condemnation. We are forever free from the covenant of works. We are free from the penalty of sin, condemnation, and sin's ruling power.

Samuel Bolton has written so clearly and powerfully on this distinction, I will quote him again:

> We are free from all that was, or is any way part of our bondage; free from Satan, from sin, from the law. . . . Whenever the Lord's jubilee is proclaimed and pronounced in a man's soul, he will never hear again of a return to bondage. He will never again come under bondage to Satan, the law, or aught else.[13]

He also teaches,

> The Gospel admits of repentance, but the law will not own it. . . . Though there may be failing in action, yet where there is truth of affection, God can own it. In the Gospel God accepts affections for actions, endeavours for performance, desire for ability. A Christian is made up of desires, of mournings, thirstings and bewailings: O that my ways were directed! O miserable man that I am! Here is Gospel perfection. . . . God can distinguish between weakness and wickedness. . . . Under the Gospel He looks not upon the weakness of saints as their wickedness, and therefore pities them. . . . The Gospel comes . . . with beseechings and with love. . . . Under the Gospel every law comes now to the saints from the mercy-seat.[14]

Christ died to free us from law, sin, and Satan. But we must remember why Christ did all this. Why did he save us, free us, and justify us? There are many reasons, but Rom 8:4 gives an oft overlooked one: "In order that the requirement of the Law might be fulfilled in us, who do not walk according to the flesh, but according to the Spirit."

One of the main reasons Christ saved us is so that we would obey him! He set us free from sin not so we can dabble in it and play with it, but so that we could fight by grace and kill it. We won't fulfill the law perfectly in this life. But slowly but surely, by his power and grace, we can begin to fulfill it. By the Holy Spirit's work in us, we can begin to be conformed to the likeness of Christ in our day-to-day lifestyle. And this brings great glory,

13. Bolton, *Bounds*, 20.

14. Bolton, *Bounds*, 42–43.

honor, and pleasure to Christ. This is why he died! This is why he rose! Live to honor such a great Savior!

Romans 8:4 is the ultimate anti-antinomian verse. If you struggle with antinomianism, I would urge you to memorize it, maybe even get a tattoo of it! The goal of salvation is not just to relish our justification but also to live out our sanctification. Serving Christ does not lead to salvation. But salvation does lead to serving Christ.

Application

Where have you lived like an antinomian? Where have you acted as though the moral law did not apply to you as a Christian? Where have you undervalued God's law in your life? Where have you not let the law direct, disclose, or drive you? Where have you minimized the power and reality of indwelling sin in your life?

We all must be honest with ourselves. We all must wake up daily ready for a battle with sin, Satan, and self. Our old man, our old ways, habits, and nature remain strong. Yet Christ in us, the hope of glory, is stronger (Col 1:27).

Most Christians will have some seasons where they are tempted to use God's great grace as a license to sin. Don't do it. It's never worth it. The pain of sin will always outlast the pleasure of sin. Thomas Brooks is helpful. "There is nothing in the world that renders a man more unlike to a saint, and more like to Satan, than to argue from mercy to sinful liberty; from divine goodness to licentiousness. This is the devil's logic. . . . Repentance *for* sin is nothing worth without repentance *from* sin."[15] Bolton agrees, "to make Christian liberty the cloak of sin: that is most damnable."[16]

True Christians will struggle mightily with sin, as we have shown. But we should not, and ultimately cannot in the long run, live in sin with peace. We must hate our sin and grieve our sin. But this alone is not enough. There must be at least some progressive turning from sin.

Christ is the lover of our soul and we should be ready, willing, and glad to give up all other affections for him, especially those for sin. Kevin DeYoung reminds us that hanging on to sin in our lives intentionally is like spiritual adultery. No wife would be okay with a mistress. Christ won't be at peace with our cherished sin. A wife would tell her husband, regarding his

15. Brooks, *Precious Remedies*, 55–57. Italics are his.

16. Bolton, *True Bounds*, 20.

mistress, "'It's me or her. You take your pick.' No one would think this sort of wife cruel, or proud, or unfair, or intolerant for making such a demand. Monogamy is her right and her husband's promise. . . . The same is true in our relationship with God. He is jealous for our exclusive commitment."[17] Do not play fast and loose with God and your sin.

Conclusion

John Owen, commenting on Rom 7:24, said,

> The nearer any one is to heaven, the more earnestly he desires to be there, because Christ is there. For the more frequent and steady are our views of him by faith, the more do we long and groan for the removal of all obstructions. . . . Now groaning is a vehement desire, mixed with sorrow, for the present want of what is desired. The desire has sorrow, and that sorrow has joy and refreshment in it; . . . and this groaning, which, when it is constant and habitual, is one of the choicest effects of faith in this life, and what we would attain to. . . . And this frame, with an intermixture of some sighs, pains, sickness of this life, is the best we can here attain to.[18]

The groaning of Rom 7:24 is about the best we can get in this life. Wretched man that I am! Who will deliver me? Christ will! Live in the tension. Live in the fight. Live in hope. Live in confidence! Live in joy!

Many people come to Christ and think they only have one or two big sins. After years of sanctification, they make real progress but realize they have dozens of different inward sins buried in their hearts. Their heart is like a gigantic room filled with small pebbles of sin as far as the eye can see. It is overwhelming.

The more a Christian truly grows, they are truly becoming more holy. Yet, they are also becoming more aware of the depths of their ongoing sin. While they may be godlier, they may feel themselves and see themselves to be more sinful than ever before. At the same time, they are growing in the knowledge of God, his goodness, grace, and holiness. The gap between their lifestyle and God's standard seems to widen experientially, even as they genuinely make progress towards a holy life.

In one sense it is depressing. But in a deeper and truer sense, it is glorious. When my view of myself gets worse and deeper, and my view of God

17. DeYoung, *Good News*, 164–65.

18. Owen, *Glory of Christ*, 181–82.

gets better and higher, the gap between him and me seemingly becomes greater. What must I do with this widening gap? Flee to Christ and cry, "Wretched man that I am! Who will set me free? Thanks be to God! Christ Jesus will."

When my view of God gets higher, and my view of myself gets lower, the view of Christ and the cross must become bigger to fill the gap. Christ becomes more significant. Christ becomes more needful and thus glorious and central in my day-to-day life and experience.

As the law breaks us of every shred and hope of self-righteousness, we are driven in deeper and fuller ways to see Christ by faith—to love and appreciate and honor Christ. As this happens, our desire and drive to obey him by grace will increase. We will have fresh Holy Spirit power and motivation to do all we can by grace to please him in all respects. The lower and deeper we go in repentance, the higher and happier we will go in true, gospel-centered worship and obedience.

Chapter 9

Adding to God's Law

WHEN SIN FIRST ENTERED the world, Satan essentially told people that God was not good. He implied God was not looking out for their best and so of course his rules for them could not be good. Thus, his law must be an unreasonable, intolerable burden. Adam, Eve, you, and I bought the lie and bit the fruit.

Immediately after their sin they felt shame, and rightfully so. Shame is not necessarily bad. What we do with our shame can be terrible. The sin after the initial sin for Adam and Eve was at least twofold.

First, they began to focus more on their relationship with one another more than their relationship with God. Their first inclination was to hide themselves from one another. They thought first to hide from other humans rather than to concern themselves with being right with God. Humans throughout time have struggled with this same reversal of priorities.

Secondly, in their relationship with one another, they did not seek honest reconciliation. Adam had sinned against Eve by not leading her and not protecting her from the snake. Eve sinned against Adam by tempting him to eat the forbidden fruit. They should have humbly confessed their sin to one another and forgiven one another. But that's not what they did. Rather, they tried to cover themselves to protect themselves. They did not trust each other. They both tried to make fig leaf aprons and loin cloths so they could not be fully seen and known by the other.

Experientially this is often the first step of legalism. We have a sense of guilt and shame. Out of concern for what other humans may think about us we try to cover ourselves up to look better than we really are. We seek to put our best foot forward. This is not primarily about the clothes we wear but the deeds we do. In these legalistic attempts we often add to God's law. We want to make ourselves look better before one another and before God. This will drive us to add things to God's law where we feel we can personally be very successful. Then as we succeed in those areas we can rest in our smug self-righteousness. At least that is what we subconsciously think. It never works in the long run.

The Pharisees of Jesus's day did this. They seemed super serious about keeping the Old Testament law as they should have been. They were actually highly selective about what they sought to keep and what they ignored. They were also super serious on keeping their own man-made interpretations. They prided themselves on being experts in God's law and the best ways to apply it. They boasted about their knowledge and practice of the law and yet failed at both. This was one of the main things Jesus confronted them about.

The Pharisees' priorities were out of whack. They exalted their own interpretation of God's word and law over God's interpretation and application. We can be guilty of this sin as well. This is a type of legalism we must guard against.

Exalt Man's Word over God's Word

Matthew 12 tells the story of Jesus and his disciples walking through a grain field on the Sabbath. The disciples were hungry and so they grabbed a snack by eating some of the grain as they walked. Pharisees saw this and complained. They accused the disciples of breaking the Sabbath.

The fourth commandment in the Ten Commandments is "Remember the sabbath day, to keep it holy. Six days you shall labor and do all your work, but the seventh day is a sabbath of the Lord your God; in it you shall not do any work" (Exod 20:8–10a). This is part of the moral law. Jews should have been serious about keeping it.

Now, even today, some Christians wrestle with the exact right application on keeping the Sabbath. Most believers believe that Sunday, the Lord's Day, is the Christian Sabbath because of the example of New Testament Christians of gathering for worship on that day. Some Christians say we should not go out to eat and make others work on the Lord's Day. Others say it is okay.

It is good and right to wrestle with wisdom in exactly how biblical laws and principles should be practically and specifically applied in our daily lives. This is part of a normal Christian life. But this normal mental wrestling match about application can turn sinful.

First, I can make my personal and practical application, everyone else's application. The Pharisees were doing this. The Bible did not specify that picking a few heads of grain for a snack was considered work and thus considered sin. But the Pharisees had decided that for them it was sin. Were they being overly scrupulous? Yes. But even worse, they were seeking to apply their scruples to others when they did not have the right to do so.

Legalists tend to be very judgmental. They tend to be hard on themselves and thus hard on others, at least in certain areas. This is a clear sign of legalism.

Let's say that you decide that based on your understanding of the Bible and church history that the best way for you to rest on Sunday is not to cook. You are a parent who cooks meals for your family all through the week. You love to serve that way, but it is also part of your daily routine that feels like work. It is often tiring and exhausting. So, on Sundays your family goes out to eat or you just eat cold food straight from the pantry or fridge. Or maybe you let the kids fend for themselves for that day. But one day out of seven you rest by ceasing from your normal labor of cooking. That may be a wise and excellent personal application of the fourth commandment for your life.

Problems will arise when you start to force your personal application on everyone else. If you teach Sunday school one week and say, "Thus saith the Lord: Thou shalt not turn on thy stove for twenty-four hours on Sundays," you are in sin. God did not say that. That personal practical application is just that. It is a personal application of an eternal principle. The principle of resting one day in seven is clear in the Bible. This application of not turning on the stove is not. Thinking of realistic applications for your personal life is wise, good, and needed. Trying to make your personal application the eleventh commandment for all people in all places at all times is arrogant and legalistic.

In some sense you are seeking to make your word equal to God's. You are highlighting your word over God's. You are putting the spotlight on your wisdom rather than his. You may not realize this or be doing it intentionally. But it is essentially what you do when you judge others in spiritual matters by your own personal standard as though it were equal to God's word.

It would not be wrong to say, "Here is a personal way I seek to obey this command in my life. . . . If it is helpful for you, feel free to use it. If not, feel free to ignore." Never make your own word equal to God's word.

When we make our personal application an application we believe all must obey, we have essentially made our application a law. We are attempting, however unaware we may be, to put our personal rules for life on par with God's holy word. It's not wrong to make personal applications of God's law for your own life. It is wrong to think they are equal or equivalent in importance to God's law. This is exactly what the Pharisees had done.

The Pharisees had come up with thirty-nine different types of work and then divided those thirty-nine types into different subcategories. In light of their personal definitions, they would define what the disciples were doing as reaping and harvesting. "By means of their hairsplitting legalism these men were constantly burying God's law under the heavy load of their traditions."[1]

Calvin comments on this passage and practice: "The Pharisees . . . were attached to outward and slight matters, so as to make holiness to consist in them entirely . . . so that one could scarcely move a finger without making the conscience tremble. It was hypocrisy, therefore, that made them so exact in trifling matters . . . the invariable practice of hypocrites to allow themselves liberty in matters of the greatest consequence, and to pay close attention to ceremonial observances."[2] When we are more concerned with what men think than what God thinks we will emphasize the outward life over the inward. When we choose a path of legalism we will necessarily focus on trifling secondary matters and neglect the weightier matters of the law.

The Pharisees would take one small verse and build mountains of supposed law and application for everyone out of it. They were adding burdens to people's backs God never intended people to bear. The Pharisees' Sabbath rules are a great example of this. D. A. Carson shows that "the rules about the Sabbath . . . are as mountains hanging by a hair, for [teaching of] Scripture [thereon] is scanty and the rules many."[3] In many areas the Bible gives a clear overriding principle such as, "Six days you shall labor and do all your work, but the seventh is a sabbath of the Lord your God; in it you shall not do any work" (Exod 20:9–10). To practically obey we must decide

1. Hendriksen, *Matthew*, 511.

2. Calvin, *Harmony*, 46.

3. Carson, *Matthew*, 279.

how to apply it personally in our lives and in the lives of those we have responsibility for to some degree. But there is always a danger of making man-made rules and treating them as divine fiat. In our lives God's word should reign supreme and not our personal applications. We must hold tightly to the command and lightly to our applications. We should seek to be as dogmatic as the Bible is, no more and no less. But to the degree that our application is not clear in the Scripture we should hold to it much more loosely.

It can seem like an impossible, overwhelming task to discern the right balance to strike in our lives between command and application. But the Bible gives us all the wisdom we need to be faithful. Deuteronomy 23:25 spoke to this issue, making a clear distinction between working with a sickle in the harvest and merely getting a snack for oneself, as the disciples were clearly doing. The Pharisees were trying to be more righteous and religious than the Bible itself. It did not work out well for them. It will not work out well for us if we follow their path.

They were more fascinated and consumed with their commentaries on God's word than they were with God's actual word and God himself. Is there anywhere in your life where you have done that? There was a theology magazine that I used to have a subscription to. But I eventually quit reading it. Because I realized that they quoted and seemed to rely more on the Westminster Confession of Faith than they did the Bible. I love the WCF and have quoted it in this book multiple times. But it does not even hold a candle to the importance the Bible ought to have in all our lives, even the most dedicated Presbyterians!

In Matt 12:2 we see the Pharisees making personal rule into a law for others to obey. Jesus responds in Matt 12:3–4 by asking them if they'd read the story of David eating consecrated bread. His point is that if they had really read, studied, and understood their Bibles well they would not be making this misapplication mistake.

David was fleeing from King Saul after he had gone crazy and decided to kill David. David was hungry, on the run, and went to the priest, asking for food. The priest gave him the bread from the tabernacle to eat, because that's all he had. The ceremonial law said this bread was only supposed to be eaten by the priests. But the Bible never condemned David for eating the bread, nor the priest for giving it. Why not?

God's law is never meant to be a burden just to make our lives harder. God's law is never about checking random boxes of obedience. So, when rituals and ceremonial law would hurt someone's life, they could be set aside. The moral law "You shall not murder" (Exod 20:13) supersedes the ceremonial law. Remember how Jesus interpreted and applied the Ten Commandments in the Sermon on the Mount. You shall not murder does not just mean do not kill people. We are meant to extrapolate from that to teach that we should love people and promote life when and where and how we can. That is what the priest did that day.

If God's written ritual law could be set aside to promote physical life, so could the Pharisees' made-up man-made applications. And so can our personal applications. Is there anywhere in your life where you have made your personal rules a law for all to obey, at least in your mind?

I know people that are incredibly serious about being on time. They see it as a way to love others and respect the time of others. That is well and good. They have a personal mantra, "If you're not fifteen minutes early, you're late!" Again, that may be a helpful personal application in their lives of love and responsibility.

But if they begin to apply that standard to all people that they interact with in a legalistic fashion they are out of bounds. Imagine the mental conversation they may have with themselves in their minds as they evaluate others by their personal standard. "Can you believe this? The guy leading the meeting just walked in at 5:58! It starts at 6 a.m. I've been here for half an hour. I had a further drive than that guy. He must be lazy or selfish. He had better have a great excuse." Again, it's fine to have a personal standard and goal that helps you practically love and respect others. But be very careful and hesitant about applying it to others.

William Perkins was a Puritan who wrote a great book on preaching. He says there are three main things the preacher should do. But he goes on to say the there is a potential fourth thing preachers may do only if they are gifted enough. Not everyone has to do it because it is so hard to do well. It is dangerous because it is so easy to do it poorly. What is his potential fourth duty for a preacher? Application. "If the preacher is suitably gifted, applying the doctrines thus explained to the life and practice of the congregation."[4] The idea is that application may be the hardest part of preaching even for those with extensive experience and training. The implication would be that making wise application for ourselves from the Bible, much less others, is a difficult task and fraught with dangers. We must be very cautious in

4. Perkins, *Art of Prophesying*, 79.

making applications of texts for other people. The danger of subtle legalism is real.

Where do you tend to be the most judgmental and condescending towards others? If you dig into your heart in that area, you are likely to find legalism. But this is the tip of the iceberg. It does not stop here.

Exalt Man's Rituals over God's Mercy

The Pharisees should not have picked a fight with Jesus over Bible interpretation and application. They were bound to lose. Jesus decided to drive home his point.

Jesus continues by noting that priests in the Old Testament were supposed to work on the Sabbath in making sacrifices to God. So, some of the holiest people broke the Sabbath every week in one sense and yet it was not sin for them. Why was that?

People were not made just to serve the law. The law was made to serve people. Most people in ancient Israel were supposed to rest from their normal labor on the Sabbath. One of the main reasons to rest from their normal work was so they could go to the tabernacle or temple and worship God. Part of that worship ceremony was sacrifices that the priests had to carry out. So, the Sabbath might actually become the busiest of work days for the priests. (This often remains true for full-time pastors of churches today! They must find another day in seven to be their "rest day.")

The point should be clear. People were not meant to serve an abstract law just for the sake of law-keeping. Rather, the law was made to serve people. It is best for people to rest one day in seven. It is best for most people to rest on the same day. It is best for most people to rest from normal labor and prioritize corporate worship on that one day of rest. But for this to be true for most people, some people, like priests in the Old Testament, had to work on the one normal day of rest. The priests were not therefore breaking the principle of Sabbath rest. They were not breaking the principle of resting and worshiping one day out of seven. Rather, they were serving God and serving his people by working on the Sabbath.

Remember, the Sabbath was a creation ordinance. God set the pattern the first week of creation. The Sabbath predates the tabernacle, the temple, and the sacrifices. The Sabbath was and is an inherently good thing meant to bless and not burden all people, meant to help and not hinder. The Sabbath was never intended to be legalistically observed. Mankind was meant to set one day aside to rest, to enjoy, and to focus on worshiping God.

Loving God with all your heart, soul, mind, and strength is primary. Corporate worship is one of the clearest ways we love God well. Loving neighbor is the second great commandment. A priest being willing to work on the Sabbath to serve so many neighbors is an act of love that fulfills the law. So, the priests were allowed to break the specific Sabbath application and not be held guilty of sinning because in doing so they were loving God and neighbor and promoting a spiritually healthy and flourishing life of worship for their neighbors.

Jesus extends the argument even further. "But I say to you, something greater than the temple is here" (Matt 12:6). What does this mean? The temple was the place where sinful man could meet with holy God and worship him and experience his forgiveness, presence, and nearness. That was why it was right for the priests to work on the Sabbath to serve the temple, so to speak. In doing so they clearly served God.

The temple was about to pass away. It would be destroyed in a few decades. The greater "temple" had already arrived. Jesus is the New Testament temple. He is the meeting place of God and man. He is where we experience grace, mercy, and worship. So, the disciples were right to spend time with him and serve him even on the Sabbath. So, even if the Pharisees wanted to accuse the disciples of working on the Sabbath by "harvesting" a snack for themselves, it did not matter. The disciples were allowed to work on the Sabbath if needed to serve Jesus, just like priests in the Old Testament could work on the Sabbath to serve the temple.

I think Jesus knew the Pharisees might not understand at this point the "Jesus is greater than the temple" argument. So, he adds, "But if you had known what this means, 'I desire compassion, and not a sacrifice,' you would not have condemned the innocent" (Matt 12:7). Jesus is referring to Hos 6:6, which the Pharisees should have known.

The bottom line is the whole point of the law is loving God and loving man. When our law-keeping becomes divorced from that, then we have missed the whole point. And that is exactly what had happened to the Pharisees. They loved outward rituals. They loved making themselves look good, pious, holy, set apart. They did not love God, and they obviously did not love people. Rather, they loved using people. They put people down and criticized others who were different than them to make themselves feel special and superior.

Even in the Old Testament God did not care that much about sacrifices and rituals. David famously said after his sin of murder and adultery, "For Thou dost not delight in sacrifice, otherwise I would give it; / Thou art not pleased with burnt offering. / The sacrifices of God are a broken spirit; / A broken and contrite heart, O God, Thou wilt not despise" (Ps 51:16–17). God is passionate about love and compassion and kindness because that is who he is. That is his heart. "God is love" (1 John 4:8, 16).

God has great compassion on people. He is moved with pity for us. And that is how he wants us to love others! This is the exact opposite of the Pharisees. They often didn't care about people; they cared about their man-made rules. They didn't care about the disciples' hunger or health. They cared about their own pride and rituals. In their sinful comparison game, they condemned men of doing wrong who had not sinned in the way they were accused.

Seemingly just to add insult to injury Jesus goes on to tell the Pharisees that he is "the Lord of the Sabbath" (Matt 12:8). By this he means, if he decides to change the rules of how the Sabbath works he can. Because he is God. He invented the Sabbath. He invented all the moral law to serve, help, and bless mankind, not to hurt, hinder, and burden people.

How does all of this relate to us living in the twenty-first century? Another way people today can add to God's law is by trying to revive Old Testament ceremonial laws or applications that may have fit in a Jewish, agrarian society two thousand years ago. But they are not for today. There are people who try to bring back and reinstate certain feasts days or dietary laws as necessary ways to obey and honor Christ today. But Col 2:16–17 is clear: "Let no one act as your judge in regard to food or drink or in respect to a festival or a new moon or a Sabbath day—things which are a mere shadow of what is to come; but the substance belongs to Christ." There were many outward rituals involved in Old Testament worship and religious living. But they pointed to Christ. Now that he has come, these things have passed away as far as having any moral value for us.

Exalt Man's Self-Righteousness over God's Salvation

Self-righteous legalists are consumed with the comparison game. They must be because they are seeking to establish their own righteous record. If their neighbor is doing better than they are then they must not be doing good enough! They often feel the need to double down and try harder.

The Pharisees hated Jesus because he was more righteous than they were and because he was taking away their power, prestige, and popularity as experts on the law. He was exposing them as sinful frauds. He humbled them and often made them look stupid in front of the crowds. They were incensed.

One wise application the Jews had for Sabbath law involved a sheep getting stuck in a ditch. If someone owned a sheep that fell and was stuck in a ditch on the Sabbath, one was allowed to "work" to pull the sheep to safety from the pit. This was commonly known and accepted teaching.

Matthew 12:9–14 tells the story of Christ going into the synagogue on the Sabbath and seeing a man with a withered hand. The Pharisees asked if it was lawful to heal the man on the Sabbath. They did not really care for the man at all. They were testing Jesus, seeing if he would break another one of their precious man-made applications, "Thou shall not heal on the Sabbath."

The Pharisees were often cold, hard-hearted, and evil. See Mark 3 as an example. They could easily see the logic of saving a poor sheep from a pit on the rest day, but they couldn't get to a place of freedom to allow a man to be healed on that same day. Their attitude was, "He can wait for tomorrow for his healing."

Mark relates the same story. Mark 3:5 tells us that Jesus was angry at the Pharisees, "grieved at their hardness of heart." They loved sheep more than men. They loved sheep because it was property that brought profit. They loved money more than men. They didn't care for men made in God's image. They did not love their neighbor as they loved themselves. In the name of keeping their man-made commandments they broke God's second great commandment, to love your neighbor.

It gets worse. Jesus heals the man, promoting life, keeping the second great commandment. The Pharisees, upon seeing this miracle, go out and begin plotting murder. They were so passionate about keeping outward, external rituals they had made up. But they had no problem committing murder. How sick, twisted, and deceived they were.

They were desperate to cover their sin, shame, and folly with their own external Sabbath-keeping, their works-based righteousness. But this story shows how shallow, hollow, and evil it all was. They were totally self-centered and blind to truth and goodness.

Jesus came to seek and save the lost. Jesus was glad to heal a poor sinner on that day and any day. The Pharisees had no answer for Jesus. They had no response. They had lost the battle. They looked like the wicked, hard-hearted fools they were that day in front of the crowds. Their power was collapsing.

They prided themselves on being the experts on God's law, in their knowledge, and practice. Yet in their pursuit of self-salvation, they misunderstood God, his law, and salvation (Rom 10:2–4). That day they met the true lawmaker and keeper. He was simultaneously more holy and just, as well as compassionate and merciful, than they could have ever imagined. They missed it. They missed him.

Application

It is easy to look at the Pharisees as stuck-up idiots. We can look down on them as smug and selfish. We would be wise to pause and see if any of their attitudes appear in our own hearts and lives.

Is there anywhere you can turn your personal application of biblical morality into a law for all people at all times? Where do people in our day tend to do this the most? In my experience it tends to be around money, politics, entertainment, food, and alcohol. I'm sure there are other areas. It's almost always emphasizing external realities over internal realities. Why is that? Legalism is very much consumed with winning the comparison game. Legalists are desperate to show off their righteousness for others to see. They are like the Pharisee standing on the street corner praying, to be seen by all (Matt 6:5).

I've heard well-meaning Christians say, "If someone wants to grow to full maturity in Christ, they have to give up all alcohol." The Bible doesn't say that. Often these people experienced powerful freedom from sin personally when they quit drinking. That is wonderful for them. It is foolish to make up a new command for all humans.

I know many who say, "I don't see how you can vote for that other political party and be a true Christian!" Maybe you don't. But be careful to not become sinfully judgmental and call something sinful that the Bible doesn't. Maybe the person did vote for the "wrong" party this time around. But maybe it was out of ignorance rather than arrogance. Be merciful and gracious in how you judge.

I've heard others say, "That man watched a movie with language I would never watch!" They dripped with an air of superiority and condescension as they spoke. Set personal standards to keep you from sin. That is wise practice. Do not assume that everyone struggles with the exact same sins in the exact same ways as you do and thus needs the exact same practices to help them fight sin.

Are there any ways that you tend to exalt some ceremony or ritual over mercy? I've known men that scream at their wives in anger about being late to church. I agree it is good to be at church on time. But I wonder sometimes if pride drives this desire in some people who just do not want to be seen as late. And even if it is a good desire, should it lead someone to scream in anger at their bride over being a few minutes late?

I've known people that boasted in the regular attendance at Wednesday night church or Sunday School. I've known people that mocked entire other denominations that did not have Sunday school. Remind me where the verse in the Bible is that commands Sunday school.

Where do you tend to wear your righteousness for others to see so you can feel better about yourself? I believe we are all tempted in this way. All of us can love box checking when it serves our purposes. We all tend to find the areas we think we naturally do better than most, and then we make too big of a deal out of that area and hold others to our own personal standards.

Let me share a personal example. Philippians 2:14 says, "Do all things without grumbling." There is good New Testament moral law. Do not grumble. My application is that when things do not go my way I need to try and not deeply sigh and show my frustration through my facial expressions, body language, and tone of voice. I think this has been a helpful personal application for me. But here is where it became legalist for a season.

One of my sons growing up was very emotionally and verbally expressive to say the least. As a child he did not have the same self-control as I did as his father. If he got in trouble, a consequence might be to lose his phone for a few hours. He would pout. I did not like his response and would come down on him in anger, sometimes yelling.

I did not see it then. But there was legalism in my heart. I took my good application to control facial expressions and turned it into a law, an unrealistic law for a teenage boy. Even if he quietly handed over his phone but rolled his eyes and stomped his feet, I was so quick to call it sin.

Here's the point. He probably was in sin in his heart. But so was I. And I was very quick to judge him harshly and severely for grumbling and complaining with his eyes, while I gave myself a pass on my outburst of anger. That is part of the self-deception of legalism. We tend to judge others harshly where they struggle and ignore where we fall. The areas we tend to stumble in, we minimize. We maximize the one to two areas we think we excel in.

The Pharisees' legalism was exposed in a conflict with Jesus and his disciples. My legalism was exposed in a conflict with my son. Are there any current hard relationships, conflicts with others, or places of the comparison game where you can see legalistic subtle tendencies in your heart? If so, confess and repent.

Conclusion

Legalism withers the soul. The Pharisees followed Jesus around but not as loyal lovers. They followed him in their sin, shame, self-righteousness, and self-centeredness, looking for a chance to accuse and condemn him. They were so desperate to keep their power and position.

They hated him because he was exposing and destroying their self-righteousness. But even his exposing of them was a form of love. It was tough love but love, nonetheless. If you are the picture of perfect health, you do not need to go see the doctor. But if something doesn't feel right, you go in for a checkup. If you have cancer but do not know it, it can kill you. If you catch it early and get treatment you may be saved. Sometimes the short-term pain and discomfort can lead to long-term healing and health.

The Pharisees were in the presence of the master Healer and Savior of souls. They were dying of a disease of pride and self-righteousness. They exalted themselves above all things so they could not see their own need, nor his solution.

They said they were the faithful keepers of the law. But they were in the presence of the one who was the embodiment of the law. He was love incarnate.

All of us have places and moments where we slip into pride, comparison, and self-righteousness. We ought to be daily following Christ around through the word and prayer just to taste and see his glory again. The more we see his glory and goodness, the more we will see our sin and shame. But this will also remind us he is a dying and rising Savior.

He is the exalted one who was willing to exalt our need for mercy over his own desires. He went to the cross to be withered under the wrath of God for us, to free us from the law of building our own righteousness apart from him.

Bow in humility, gratitude, and awe in your heart. Worship his mercy afresh. Enjoy the goodness of such a Savior who came to heal us finally and fully from the disease of sin. He loves to bless, not burden. He heals us and helps us and never hurts us in the long run. He came to seek and save the lost, not to scorn. Let us go and, by grace, do likewise.

Chapter 10

Subtracting from the Law

This book is examining the role of moral law in the Christian life. This chapter is looking specifically at legalism. In the last chapter we considered how adding to God's law is a form of legalism. In this chapter we build on that idea. The title at first may sound like a type of antinomianism rather than a type of legalism. Legalism is often subtle and tricky. Sometimes in the name of exalting the law it actually subtracts from the law.

Remember, when sin first entered the world, people's first response was to hide from each other behind their own good works: fig leaf aprons of their own making. Soon after that they heard God in the garden. Then they ran and hid from him in fear. Their attempts to hide from one another were not very successful. Their attempt to hide from God was laughable. Pharisees and all legalists are still attempting to hide from God to some degree. We will look at three ways this is done. Legalists *refocus*, *reinterpret*, and ultimately *reduce* the law.

Refocus the Law

Luke 11 tells the story of a Pharisee who seems to have some interest in Jesus. He invites Jesus to his house for lunch. As we saw in the last chapter, Pharisees had added to God's law in many ways. One of their additions is they prescribed ceremonial hand-washings they considered necessary before any meal. The thinking behind the washing was, "What if I accidently touched a gentile in the market today or touched something a gentile had touched? If I touch and eat food with those same hands, I would be ceremonially unclean." In this fearful thinking they developed an elaborate, showy way to wash hands. They pointed their fingers up and poured water over them. Then they turned them down and poured more water. The Bible never taught this. The Jewish Mishnah were recordings of rabbis' ancient oral teachings. William Hendriksen says, "The Pharisees continued to advocate strict compliance with the rules laid down by the prominent rabbis of former days. . . . Ever so many minute ceremonial regulations regarding hundreds of matters were being constantly handed down as if salvation itself depended on all-out obedience. . . . They stressed human regulations at the expense of divine ordinances!"[1]

There is obviously nothing wrong with washing your hands before lunch. There is something terribly wrong if you attach spiritual significance to it. Are there extra biblical rules or standards to which you have assigned spiritual meaning?

Hendriksen speculates out that the Pharisees likely insisted on such trifling issues as "a cover for inner insecurity."[2] Just like Adam and Eve in the garden, when a human being is not right with God there will be a deep sense of insecurity that makes us want to run and hide from God. There will be inward fear before our own conscience. When we are not resting deeply in the finished work of Christ for us, we will look to our own good works. And they will never be enough. Our best days and deeds will never make us feel secure in our walk with God. There will always be a gnawing sense of "my best isn't good enough!" When we feel that inner mental wrestling match, what do we often do? We refocus on something else.

We become like a magician that tries to distract his client with his left hand while the right hand performs the trick. All people have an inward sense of how sinful and guilty we are before God (Rom 1:18–32). We have some sense of God's justice and the impossibility of us ever closing the gap between him and our sinful selves. The best way to fix this in our own strength (or at least attempt to fix it) is to quit trying or to at least change the rules of the game.

When my kids were young, we played a lot of driveway basketball. Two of my sons were competitive and took it very seriously. Maybe the older one said at the beginning, "We are playing to fifteen." But then as the game progresses and he sees that he is losing, he may quickly say, "We said we're playing to twenty-one, right?" The goal is to win at all costs. If rules must be changed midstream to do so, so be it. In a similar way, we can seek

1. Hendriksen, *Luke*, 637–39.
2. Hendriksen, *Luke*, 644.

to change the rules of the salvation and security game, at least in our own heads. The problem is it never works.

As the Pharisees inwardly critiqued Jesus, he knew their thoughts and responded, "You Pharisees clean the outside of the cup and of the platter, but inside of you, you are full of robbery and wickedness. You foolish ones, did not He who made the outside make the inside also?" (Luke 11:39–40). Biblically, to call someone a fool is to say they live as a practical atheist. You act and think as though God were not real or not involved at all in life. You live as though God does not see and so you can sin with impunity. Jesus rebukes these men to say, "You think God only cares about externals and not internals?" He goes on to say they are very sinful inwardly, very greedy, full of love for money to the point that they steal it.

What exactly is Jesus thinking of in accusing the Pharisees of robbery? We are not sure, but he likely has in mind that they were not generous and did not provide for the poor as the Old Testament commands. "But give that which is within as charity, and then all things are clean for you" (Luke 11:41). He may mean give from your heart to the poor. He may mean give the food in the dishes to the poor. Either way, the meaning is that loving your neighbor by giving to the poor is a true sign of salvation and a changed life. Only by a supernatural inward change can someone truly be clean before God. It will never come through ceremonial cleansing alone.

The Pharisees did not want to be sacrificial, loving, and generous. That's too hard, too costly, too all encompassing. So, they decided to make up hand-washing services that were more manageable and serviceable. Subconsciously they may have known these outward deeds wouldn't help them much with God. But it could help them with poor, ignorant people who might hold them in awe. If we can't win with God, we will often try to win the righteousness game by comparing ourselves and impressing others. We refocus the true nature of God's law.

Reinterpret the Law

The Pharisees did not just refocus on outward, man-made rules to cover their neglect of more important laws; they also tried to reinterpret the law. We might say they attempted to rightsize the law. The law of God, love God and man, was overwhelming. So, Pharisees and many of us today try to cut it down to size, to something we can handle.

There's a story of a boy shooting arrows at the wall of a barn. He would shoot one arrow at the side of the barn. Wherever it landed he would paint a bull's-eye target around it. He figured out what he could realistically do first. Then he later determined that was his goal. That's how Pharisees think in this situation.

In Luke 11:42 Jesus warns the Pharisees of God's coming wrath. He notices they have become experts in tithing from the small plants in their garden. The Old Testament clearly taught tithing, and the Pharisees did it. But they took it to another level. Even if it meant counting one out of every ten leaves or seeds, they were meticulous to tithe. The Bible did not command that level of strictness. But Jesus essentially says that is fine if you want to go the extra mile in tithing. But what you can't do is focus so much on tithing and think that it is a covering for more important issues such as love and justice. Again, it is likely that Jesus specifically thinks of loving and helping the poor here.

The Bible is supremely clear that some laws are more important than others. Jesus spoke of the greatest commandment and the second-greatest commandment. So, we should major in the majors and minor in the minors. It does not mean to ignore minor or secondary laws. It does mean putting them and keeping them in their proper place.

Modern day equivalents to the pharisees often have a dual motive for this type of rightsizing the law. It makes them feel better with themselves. It also makes them look better in front of others. If I love God internally with all my heart, no one can see my heart. But if I am meticulous about tithing and washing my hands, others can observe that. I can get credit at the human level and have a sense of blessed self-assurance! If what one really wants is approval of man more than approval from God, what good are internal realities other people cannot even see?

Imagine I left a sixteen-year-old son to babysit younger siblings. I told him, "Mainly keep everyone safe and be kind and loving to your siblings. If there's time after they all go to bed, please wash the dishes as well."

If I come home three hours later and find the kitchen cleaned meticulously, all dishes polished, I might be grateful. But if I then learn that he was a jerk to his siblings, my gratitude over dishwashing will greatly diminish. If his younger siblings are crying in their beds and tell me that their older brother screamed at them and wouldn't let them watch TV because he wanted to play video games all night, I will not be pleased. It won't matter how much my oldest son boasts in his dishwashing performance; I will be grieved by his lack of love for his siblings. And thus it is with Father God when we major in minors and neglect to love our neighbors.

Every human only has so much mental capacity. If I maximize my mental energy focused on secondary issues, I will not have what I need to focus on the primary issues. If I am consumed with performing outward acts to impress other human beings, I will not have the time or capacity to focus on loving God with all my heart, soul, mind, and strength or on loving my neighbor as myself.

Jesus exposes the Pharisees in Luke 11:43. He says that what they really love is not God. They are not primarily concerned with what God thinks about them. Rather, they are consumed with what others think of them. They are obsessed with the praise of man. This is so much of the heart of legalism. Can you see any of this in yourself?

Numbers 19:11–22 teaches that Jews would be ceremonially unclean if they touched a dead body. Considering this, the Jewish people often marked graves very clearly so they would not accidently walk over them. In Luke 11:44 Jesus says the Pharisees are like hidden graves. Jesus means that average Jewish citizens came to the Pharisees seeking knowledge about God's law, etc. The Jews thought they would be helped by the Pharisees who were supposedly experts on God's law. In truth, coming to the Pharisees was like accidently walking over a grave. The Pharisees were so mixed up and confused they pushed people further from God. By listening to and following the teachings of the Pharisees, people were further from God rather than closer.

Reduce the Law

Lawyers in ancient Israel were professionals in charge of interpreting God's law. They came up with most of the interpretations and claimed following their applications was more important than following the law itself. Pharisees followed their interpretations. Many Pharisees were lawyers and vice versa, but not all of them were both. In Luke 11:45, a lawyer speaks up to say, essentially, "You may not mean to, Jesus, but we are personally insulted by your teaching as well."

Jesus turns his verbal assault on them as well, insinuating, "You lawyers do the same things. All my rebukes to the Pharisees apply to you as well." The lawyers made up so many fake applications of the law. They burdened Jewish people who truly wanted to obey and please God. They buried God's word and made it obscurer rather than clearer. A Bible scholar's job is to make the truth clearer and easier to understand and apply. They did the opposite. Further, they didn't even practice what they preached.

They often came up with loopholes for themselves. "You can swear by this, but not by this." See Matt 23:16–22 for an example. It is like the U.S. Congress passing laws that others must obey, but the lawmakers themselves are exempt. It's like an accountant who demands that others pay their fair share of taxes but finds special ways where they themselves do not have to. Some environmentalists rail against others in society for polluting the environment but then fly on private planes regularly to their environmental meetings and do not feel guilty about their own carbon pollution.

Preachers can be very guilty of this. I have been. It can sound very powerful, convicting, and spiritual to make a strong radical statement in a sermon that convicts and impresses others. "Wow! This preacher really brings the heat!" some might say after the sermon. But if I, or anyone else, passionately pounds the pulpit about an application of God's word that I don't keep, I'm a fraud at some level, more concerned with man's approval than God's.

What about the preacher that talks about obeying the speed limit as an application of Rom 13:1–5 and then regularly speeds? What about the pastor who condemns watching R-rated movies but then indulges himself in them? What about a pastor who extols bold friendship evangelism but then rarely if ever practices it himself? It is easy to fall into.

Legalists add man-made rules to God's rules. Legalists make man-made application equal to God's law. But they also subtract from God's law, because practically speaking they do not obey all that God wants them to obey. They are too busy fulfilling their silly man-made laws to give adequate time to God's ways. The weightier matters of the law like charity, justice, and loving God and neighbor get lost and neglected. It's never good when God's law gets lost in the shuffle of our own applications. Legalists exalt man-made minutia and subtract from God's law the weightiest matters.

Application

Is there any way you find yourself trying to refocus the law in your own life? I've seen some Christian ministers get so focused on physical health that they become passionate advocates for certain diet fads or vitamins. The Bible does teach that we should be a good steward of our physical body.

Drunkenness and gluttony are sins. We should all think about the practical implications of these commands and warnings. If I decide to take a certain multivitamin every day, that may be wise for me. If you decide to cut processed foods out of your diet, that may be best for you as well. If you and I go on a crusade to rebuke people for not following our personal physical diets, we are immature at best and arrogant at worst. God cares about your physical body. He cares more about your heart attitude and spirit that drives your applications.

Are there ways you attempt to reduce and rightsize the law into a more manageable system? What about someone who tithes on all money they receive, even if it was a birthday gift? Not only that, but they make sure to let everyone know about their extra-scrupulous tithing practices. I've known people who boasted about the fact that their kids rarely, if ever, miss any youth night church events. They were also a little snooty, ornery, tight with their money, and hard to work with. Are we ever boasting about good things that are not necessary things? Have we tried to boil down true righteousness to some outward behaviors we can manage?

Is there anywhere in life where you knowingly break God's clear word? Are there ever times where you try to cover over your guilty conscience by extra man-made obedience? Do you ever try to emphasis certain practices primarily so others can see you doing them and you can get "extra credit" for them?

Here's a great question to wrestle with. When's the last time you let the law of God have its way with you? We are often like the lawyer who is offended by Jesus's clear teaching and doesn't like it, and so we attempt to push back in some way. But a mature believer will let God's word cut and convict. It may hurt, but I should not be insulted. I should be humbled and glad. I should welcome the convicting work of God's law in my life.

Very recently I heard someone teach on what the Bible says about ministering to the least of these, to prisoners and such. I also read in God's word about the importance of giving money to the poor. I was convicted. I tithe to my church and give to other missionaries and different organizations. But I give very little to ministries focused directly on the poor. At that time I had a friend in prison and a mother-in-law in a nursing home. I felt I was not visiting them as often as I should. At first there was something in my heart that wanted to boast and brag. I wanted to boast about all the money I do give. I wanted to brag about and rest in all the other ministry work I do with people in my ministry and church. All of this was inward. In a subtle way, I was trying to reduce and refocus God's word so that it would fit the lifestyle I was already living, and I could feel right with myself.

By God's grace I was able to shut my inner lawyer's mouth and let the Holy Spirit have his way with me. I began to pray that God would make clear a ministry that ministered directly to the poor that I could start regularly giving to. I got out my calendar and planned a visit to my mother-in-law and my friend in prison. It ended up being a sweet time alone with the Lord. My gut reaction was to push back. The Holy Spirit helped me humble myself, listen to the word, and repent.

Loving the poor and needy is big on God's heart. It's obviously not big enough on mine. I was the one who needed to change to conform myself to God's law. I did not need to try and conform God's law to suit the lifestyle I was comfortable living.

Maybe the best question we should all wrestle with considering all of this is "Whose approval do we most want?" Do we most want to impress other people? Do we most want to feel comfortable with ourselves? Or deep down, do we really want to please and honor God above all? What do my actions say about these questions? Who am I really serving with my law-keeping?

Conclusion

The last rebuke Christ had for these Pharisees and lawyers in this interaction was that they acted as though they truly respected the Old Testament prophets, but they really did not. They built elaborate tombs to honor the men and attended to their graves. But they did not live according to their teaching (Luke 11:47–52).

Billy Graham is widely known as the greatest evangelist of the twentieth century. He famously preached basic gospel sermons to crowds of many non-Christians around the world. Many people came to Christ through his ministry.

Imagine if there was a group of people who talked often and loudly about how much they loved and respected Billy Graham. They often traveled to North Carolina (his home state) to pay homage to his final resting place. Maybe they even sing songs and write books about Billy Graham. There's only one problem. They never share their faith. They never talk to non-Christians. They've never preached a sermon to a lost person. They really do not even care about their neighbor's eternal destiny. Would these people be truly honoring Billy Graham even as they took flowers to his grave on their annual pilgrimage? They would not.

Deep down many legalists know they cannot really earn God's approval, so they have given up trying. Earning man's approval is much easier and more realistic. They set their sights on a more manageable goal. In the process they reduce the law, reinterpret it, and refocus it by subtracting all parts they do not like or cannot personally handle.

The Pharisees and lawyers of Jesus's day could not handle obeying the Old Testament prophets. The prophets who wrote much of the Jewish Scripture talked much about loving God and neighbor. They spilled a lot of ink on giving to the poor and treating the needy with justice and kindness.

The greatest evidence these legalists gave that they did not obey the prophets of old messages is that they had the greatest prophet of all time standing in front of them, looking into their eyes, speaking into their ears, and they resisted. They were overwhelmed by the teaching of Christ. Rather than let his teaching humble and break them, they hardened themselves against him. They should have been driven to fall at his feet and beg mercy and grace. Rather we are told they went out and began to plot against him (Luke 11:53–54).

The saving grace in this passage is that Christ is the embodiment and fulfillment of all that he taught. The Pharisees' man-made rules and applications were ultimately self-serving, self-aggrandizing as well. They were attempting to make themselves look good in front of others and thus feel better about themselves. They took God's word and boiled it down to more realistic and attainable bite-size pieces they could accomplish and flaunt in front of the public while they did it.

One of the many problems with this reshaping of the law is that it often became a greater burden for average citizens. It often made things more confusing for someone who was not an expert in all the Pharisees' explanations. The Pharisees and lawyers often did not love their neighbors as they loved themselves. If others were confused, that was their fault. The Pharisees were chasing their own glory and fame. Others could be damned, for all they cared.

Jesus's law-keeping was not selfish. He kept the law to honor the Father and to serve his people. The Lord Jesus did not come to add burdens to our lives. He knows we are already overwhelmed and weighed down with sin and shame. He came to take the burden of sin off us, carry it to the cross, and pay for it fully and finally there!

Christ earned the Father's approval for us. He did what we could never do if we lived for a thousand years. Now we can listen to God's moral law. We can let it cut, convict, and have its way with us. We can be humble, broken, yet glad before it. We are already free if we are in Christ. We are saved and secure by his great grace. Now we can hear his words not as condemnation but as instruction. It is not a command to be sinlessly perfect or else. Rather, it is fatherly wisdom and the counsel of an older brother. It is a word of kindness and love. His moral law now comes to us sweetly to guide and instruct in the best ways to live. He shows us how to flourish personally, how to best love others, and how to enjoy honoring him in all we say, think, desire, feel, and do.

Even when the law seems loud and hard, it should never drive a Christian away from Christ. Rather, it should drive us closer to him. His word that convicts should humble us to rest more fully in the finished work of Christ. As we are motivated to appropriate his words and power to love him and others, we should be freed from the burden of worrying about what others think about us. We are not living for their approval. We are living for his approval, and we already have it, secured in Christ.

Chapter 11

Earning from the Law

I WROTE ONLY ONE chapter specifically to combat antinomianism in this book. This will be the third on legalism. Why is that? Legalism can be more subtle and thus harder to detect. There are many ways Christians and professing Christians can use the law of God in wrong ways in their lives.

Legalists will add to God's law. Sometimes they add their own man-made applications and treat it as divine. Other times they resurrect Old Testament ceremonies that have been fulfilled and surpassed in Christ. This often has to do with trying to impress others with their outward displays of "righteousness."

Legalists will also subtract from God's law. They will rightsize it so they can maintain some form of self-righteousness. This often has to do with trying to make themselves feel right before God. They want to be able to hang on to some sort of dignity before him but also in front of others.

In this chapter we will look at how legalists seek to earn from the law. This often has to do with making themselves feel secure. They are seeking to quiet their conscience. Augustine said that the Jews in large part sought Christ but missed him because they "were preoccupied with their own merits."[1]

Paul wrote Galatians to defend the concept of salvation by grace alone through faith alone. Salvation is not by our work to any degree. He spent much of the first two chapters sharing his personal testimony as well as some important church history. More of the didactic teaching begins in chapter 3. In the first five verses of chapter 3 he will show that faith *saves*, *secures*, and *sanctifies*.

1. Augustine, *City*, 644.

Faith Saves

Paul teaches that when you have heard faithful gospel preaching it is as though you stood at the foot of the cross and watched him die for sinners. "You foolish Galatians, who has bewitched you, before whose eyes Jesus Christ was publicly portrayed as crucified" (Gal 3:1). The hearers of Paul's letter had not been at Calvary the day Christ died. But by faith, they had seen Christ die for them. The members of this church heard the gospel of grace and placed their faith in Christ. But now, years later, they act as though Christ had not died for them or his death was not sufficient for their salvation.

False teachers had come from Jerusalem and taught that true salvation did not rest in faith in Christ alone. Faith in Christ was necessary, but not sufficient, they taught. Old Testament ceremonial law must be added to it. A gentile must become a Jew to experience all the benefits of Christ. Faith in Christ was helpful, but so was circumcision. Both were needed to fully experience salvation and assurance. Some of the Galatian church members had started to believe in the false teachings. Paul tells them they have been tricked and fooled. They should have known better.

He goes back to the fundamentals of salvation. He asks, "Did you receive the Spirit by works of the Law, or by hearing with faith?" (Gal 3:2). He asks them to remember when they were first saved and indwelled by God's Spirit. How did that happen? Were there any works they had to perform? Or did they merely hear the message of grace and believe? The answer is obvious. They heard about and trusted in Christ alone and were saved.

It is important to remember that even faith itself is not meritorious work that saves me. Faith is the instrument that connects me to Christ. But Christ alone saves. I do not trust in my faith, but in Christ to save. Kevin DeYoung is very helpful: "Faith is not what God finds acceptable in us. In fact, strictly speaking, faith itself does not justify. Faith is only the instrument by which we embrace Christ. . . . It is the object of our faith that matters. . . . Believe in Christ with all your heart, but don't put your faith in your faith. Your experience of trusting Christ will ebb and flow. So be sure to rest in Jesus Christ and not your faith in Him."[2]

The most blatant and lethal type of legalism is to think that I am saved by my own work. Even if I think I am saved by the strength of my faith, that is a type of legalism. True salvation is about looking totally away from

2. DeYoung, *Good News*, 117.

myself, helpless and dependent fully on another, Christ, to save me from myself, my sins, and the wrath of God.

In all my life, I have never met anyone who believes they are saved 100 percent by their own works. But I have met many who believe they are saved by some combination of God's grace and their good works. This is one of if not the most common errors about salvation. Many false churches teach this. Many individuals subtly feel and believe this though they may not articulate it this clearly. This error must be avoided at all costs.

The true gospel is salvation by God's good grace *alone*! If you try to add any of your own works to it, even only 1 percent, you have ruined free grace. God's grace and our works in justification are antithetical like oil and water. They do not mix.

If someone stops you on the street and says he will give you a free lunch for your child, that is great news! But if he goes on to say, you must buy an adult meal first with your own money and then the free child's meal is added, it's not fully free. It's not a gift with no strings attached. There is a condition. The prerequisite must be supplied by your own hard-earned dollars. This is not how salvation works. God does not promise to save us "freely by grace" if we first do a few small, good works like go to church, get baptized or circumcised, etc.

A true free lunch is when someone hands me a coupon for a free Chick-fil-A sandwich. No purchase necessary. Show up, hand in the coupon, get the food. That is free. An even better illustration would be someone just walked up and put the sandwich in my hand. I literally did nothing. I stood there passively and received. That is grace. Many of us know this truth and may even die for it. But the implications at times can be fuzzy.

Faith Secures

Paul continues his logical argument. "Are you so foolish? Having begun by the Spirit, are you now being perfected by the flesh?" (Gal 3:3). The Galatians should be clear that they entered salvation and Christ by sheer grace alone. But there is another type of legalism we are all prey to. We can believe we are initially justified by God's grace apart from our works. But then we can begin to believe if are to stay in Christ and grow in Christ we must add some merit. This may be a lighter type of legalism, but it is still legalism.

Paul asks the Galatians to consider, do they grow in grace because of the Spirit's work in them or because of their own man-made efforts? There are some denominations that teach salvation by grace alone through faith alone. But then they teach that you can lose this salvation if you sin badly enough. They essentially say, "You got in by grace, but you can get out by works." Do you see the problem in this logic? If I can get out by doing bad enough works, then there is some sense in which I must stay in salvation through doing enough good works or at least avoiding enough evil deeds. If my salvation's security is based to any degree on my law-keeping, I am now back to a works-based salvation, no matter what I may say. According to this view my work plays a necessary, essential role in securing my salvation. But this is not the gospel.

This works-based security breaks down in so many ways. If I was dead in sin and made alive by Christ's grace alone but then lose my salvation by works, how can I come back to Christ? Do I come back to salvation through some new good works, to cover the old bad ones? The truth is I am saved by grace alone, I am secured by grace alone, and I persevere ultimately by God's good grace alone.

If we believe that we stay in a state of salvation to some degree by our works, then almost certainly, subtly, internally, we also believe we got into the state of salvation to some degree by our own good deeds. This goes against one of the main themes of the whole Bible. There are some verses that sound as though someone can lose their salvation. But they must be interpreted by all the other verses that so clearly teach that one cannot lose their salvation, such as Matt 7:19–23, John 6:37–44, Rom 8, Phil 1:6, and 1 John 2:19.

Galatians 3:4 could be construed to teach that losing salvation is possible: "Did you suffer so many things in vain—if indeed it was in vain?" At first glance, this may seem to say the church members in Galatia had been saved and suffered for their faith in Christ but now were losing their salvation. So, all their suffering for Christ had been in vain. But the best understanding is that there may have been people in the church who professed faith in Christ, suffered for that profession, but in truth, never really had genuine salvation. I'll quote this again because it has been so personally helpful to me. Frank Barker, the founding pastor of Briarwood Presbyterian Church in Birmingham, Alabama, used to say, "Faith that fizzles before the finish was false from the first." This quote brings so much clarity. If someone "leaves the faith" they never truly had the faith in a saving, secure way.

The questions that must be wrestled with are: "Did I ever truly trust in Christ? Am I trusting in him now?" It's not right or helpful to think, "Did I lose my salvation?" because biblically that is impossible. When Paul says "if indeed it was in vain," it seems he believes the Galatians are genuine believers. He does believe they are struggling and in a state of confusion though.

Faith Sanctifies

Paul continues: "Does He then, who provides you with the Spirit and works miracles among you, do it by the words of the Law, or by hearing with faith?" (Gal 3:5). Paul believes the Holy Spirit is living in the Galatians to whom he writes. When he speaks of miracles, he may mean such things as healing, etc. But he likely also refers to the miracle of a changed life. The Holy Spirit comes into a believer to make us alive in Christ and then to start a lifelong journey of being conformed to the image of Christ. We begin to bear the fruit of the Holy Spirit Paul discusses in Gal 5:22–23.

What is the main reason the Holy Spirit sanctifies his people? What is the foundational reason or the meritorious cause? Is it just because we have trusted in God's word and promises? Or is it because we are doing our best to obey and earn God's favor? This can be a confusing point, because Christians are meant to work in conjunction with the Holy Spirit to bring about the fruit of the Holy Spirit in our lives. For instance, Gal 5:25 instructs us to "walk by the Spirit." There are things I am supposed to do, decisions I am supposed to make to obey God's word.

My personal obedience to God's word may be a functional cause (not the only one, but one among others), one of the reasons that I am growing in Christlikeness. But it is never a foundational or meritorious cause. It is never a cause in the sense that I am earning something from God. God never looks down from heaven, sees me trying my best to obey, and says, "Well, he's trying his best. He deserves some help. Let's give him more power for holiness today." I can never earn anything from God in heaven, even with my best works, other than his wrath, anger, and condemnation.

The only meritorious cause I have for anything good from God is the grace of Christ. God gives all good things to his Son. Because I am in Christ, I deserve to share in these good things with him. Salvation, sanctification, and glorification are all ultimately done because of God's sheer grace alone!

Now at first glance this can seem to promote antinomianism. It would be easy to stop here and say, "Well, God is going to sanctify me no matter what, based on sheer grace, so I can do whatever the heck I want and all will be well. I'll grow no matter what." But that is obviously against the whole tenor of the Bible. Once we are saved and in right relationship with God, he wants us to use our efforts and willpower to work in conjunction with the Holy Spirit. He does not want us to resist, quench, grieve or be stiff-necked towards the Spirit's work in our lives. See Acts 7:51, Eph 4:30, and 1 Thess 5:19. He wants us to humbly comply with the Holy Spirit. But even on our best days, our works do not earn or merit anything from God.

Foundationally we are sanctified, meaning made holy, because of faith alone, but functionally by faith plus works. An explanation will help dispel the confusion. Remember Josh 6 where God commanded the Israelites to march around the walled city of Jericho. They marched around the wall for six days in silence. On the seventh day they marched and shouted, and the wall fell. God had commanded them to do this. They obeyed. Their obedience mattered. We could rightly say their marching and shouting was instrumental to the victory over the city, but not meritorious. Obedience was functional, not foundational. Our good works and best deeds after justification are likewise instrumental to sanctification. They are not meritorious.

We do not find the Israelites boasting in their efforts to conquer Jericho. Joshua 10:16 says, "The Lord has given you the city." They rightly gave all glory, honor, praise, and credit to God for his supernatural power doing the work they could not do. They did not attribute the victory to how well they marched nor how loud they shouted. Yet neither did they act as though their obedience was insignificant. They had an instrumental part to play in the victory, but not a meritorious one. Likewise, we have an instrumental role to play in our sanctification but never a meritorious one. You would never find an Israelite soldier later saying, "My shouts knocked down that wall!" They knew better. Neither should we ever find a Christian saying, "My good works and hard efforts at sanctification have guaranteed my forward progress in faith!"

Christians would be helped if we took the words "merit," "earn," and "deserve" totally out of our vocabulary when it comes to our relationship with God. Christ earned salvation for me. Christ has merited my sanctification. Christ deserves that his people be sanctified. But I, of myself, have done none of that. And neither have you. On our best days, empowered by the Holy Spirit, we can still not merit anything from God except anger, wrath, fury, and hell. Because all that I do is still tainted by indwelling sin, I cannot be sinlessly perfect even for one second. But God does call me to obey, just as a good father calls an adopted son to obey. The good father is not asking his adopted son to earn his adoption or to pay the father back.

But now that the father and son are in this adoptive relationship, the only right response of the son is joyful obedience.

The Father essentially says to us, "Obedience by faith is the place of blessing. That is where I delight to pour out my power and grace, when you choose to lovingly obey me." James 4:6: "God . . . gives grace to the humble." This does not mean that humility earns grace from God. Rather, it means God likes humility. He enjoys it. He delights to pour out his favor and power on those who choose to humble themselves before him. Christ has purchased the grace for his people. God decides when, where, and how to pour out these riches on us.

Imagine one of my sons just turned sixteen years old. I teach him to drive. I buy him a car. I put gas in the car. And then, for his first solo drive, I ask him to drive to the gas station and buy me a Coke. I tell him I'll give him five dollars if he can do this on his own without getting into a wreck. He comes home ten minutes later, hands me the Coke and says, "Pay up dad! I earned my five dollars." How might I respond?

I'd likely say, "Son, I'm happy to give you the five dollars because I promised, and you did what I said. But you didn't earn it." It would be much better and more accurate if my son said, "Dad, here's the Coke you asked me to get. Will you please keep your promise and give me the five dollars?" It is a different attitude. There is humility rather than a swagger. The first example of the son's demand sounds meritorious and entitled. The second sounds humble and trusting. What's your heart attitude before Christ?

Christians operate with the Lord on the basis of his promises to us in Christ. We never operate with him based on our own merits or what we have earned or deserved. Keeping this distinction clear in our minds is crucial.

Justification is monergistic. This means it is the act of one person, not a partnership. It is an act of God's free grace alone. I am entirely passive when God declares me righteous in the cosmic courtroom of the universe. As the hymn by Elvina M. Hall says, "Jesus paid it all, / All to him I owe; / Sin had left a crimson stain, / He washed it white as snow."[3]

Sanctification is synergistic. It is a word of God's free grace. But I am very active. I partner with him in this ongoing work of bringing the fruit of Christ's life to bear in my own life. I am active. But I am not an earner. I am moving, but I bring no merit. I do deeds, but I never deserve his grace.

3. Hall, "Jesus Paid It All."

The older son in the parable of the two sons had a works-based mentality. He yells at the father, "I've worked so hard for you, but you never gave me one goat for myself. But you slaughtered the fattened calf for my younger sinful brother?!" (See Luke 15:29–30 for an exact quote.) His attitude shows he felt like the father was in debt to him. After all his years of service, at minimum he had earned the right to one goat.

The father's response is brilliant. "My child, you have always been with me, and all that is mine is yours" (Luke 15:31b). The father speaks to him not of works and earning and deserving but rather of relationship. "Son, I am your father! You already have a right by relationship to all the wealth that is mine. All you had to do was ask in faith!"

Jesus told the disciples the right attitude to have about all the hard work and suffering they would do for the Lord. "So you too, when you do all the things which are commanded you, say, 'We are unworthy slaves; we have done only that which we ought to have done" (Luke 17:10). I can never claim to earn anything from God's divine grace. He gives it to his children lavishly because he enjoys doing it. He has promised to bless our obedience. We are wise to cash in on that promise. We are foolish to ever think that makes him our debtor.

The consistent teaching of the Bible is that salvation starts and ends by faith. Matthew Henry, commenting on Rom 1:16–17, says, "From the first faith, by which we are put into a justified state, to later faith, by which we live; from faith engrafting us into Christ, to faith deriving virtue from him as our root . . . there is faith justifying us . . . there is faith maintaining us. Faith is all in all, both in the beginning and progress of a Christian life. It is increasing, continuing, persevering faith."[4]

Romans 7:18 and 8:13 teach that I do not have the power to obey and to kill sin in myself. I must look away from myself to God. I must trust the power of the Holy Spirit to enable me to obey and put sin to death.

Galatians 5:6 describes sanctification as "faith working through love." Yes, I work, but's it is my faith in Christ, working for me. I work, but my power and motivation to work all come through my faith in Christ.

Philippians 2:13–14 may be the most helpful passage to strike the right balance: "Just as you have always obeyed, not as in my presence only, but now much more in my absence, work out your salvation with fear and trembling; for it is God who is at work in you, both to will and to work for His good pleasure." Left to myself, I cannot do anything good. But by faith

4. Henry, *NIV Matthew Henry Commentary*, 564.

alone I am attached to Christ. I am spiritually married to him. I am joined to him as a branch is joined to the life-giving vine. He works in me. He enables me to obey. He gives me desire to obey. But I must work as unto the Lord. I must work out into reality in my practical life what he works in me. He is changing me from the inside out, but I must work in conjunction with the Holy Spirit to bring the fruit to bear. I must put real effort and energy into partnering with the Holy Spirit. I must take this task very seriously.

Philippians 4:13 teaches the same thing: "I can do all things through Him who strengthens me." He gives me the power to obey. I bring that power to bear on my life day by day. I appropriate his power. The Holy Spirit lives and works in me. I live by complete dependence on him. I can never boast in my own effort or work.

Colossians 1:29b strikes the balance so well: "I labor, striving according to His power, which mightily works within me." Why can this balance be so hard to understand, practice, and even articulate in the Christian life? Because there is a ditch on both sides of the road: legalism on one side, where I overemphasize my responsibility and effort, and antinomianism on the other side, where I downplay my involvement. Samuel Bolton wisely said, "It is hard to perform all righteousness and rest in none; hard to be in duties in respect of performance, and out of duties in respect of dependence."[5] By God's grace I am to do all I can to perform all the duties conforming to obedience of God's moral law. But I must fully remember that I never rest in my own obedience. I am never dependent on my own performance for my standing before God. Only Christ can secure my standing eternally before the Father. There is a type of obedience that is grace-filled and not "legal obedience."[6]

A rowboat is a good picture of legalism. If I'm in a rowboat alone, it is 100 percent up to me if I make any progress crossing the lake. A legalist often feels that if they are to make any progress in the sanctification process, it is all up to them or at least mostly up to them. They must work hard, with blood, sweat, and tears, to grow. The Holy Spirit seemingly plays little to no role.

A speedboat is a good picture of an antinomian. I can turn the engine on with a key, push the throttle fully forward, and make swift progress across the lake. I can take a nap, and the boat will continue to function regardless of my actions. I am minimally involved if at all. The engine,

5. Bolton, *True Bounds*, 70.

6. Bolton, *True Bounds*, 10.

representing God, does all the work regardless of my effort. Let go and let God! Let go and let the ski boat drive! An antinomian often feels it would be legalistic to strive for holiness. The antinomian feels they can totally relax and trust God to grow them up in Christ regardless of any effort they put into the process.

A sailboat is a great illustration of the Christian life in healthy balance. There is work to be done. Sails must be raised and turned in certain ways at certain times. But if the wind does not blow you will not move, regardless of how perfectly you have trimmed the sails. If the wind blows perfectly, but your sails are not prepared to catch the wind, you may not move at all, or very little. But when a wise sailor adjusts his sails just right and the wind comes along, his boat will make speedy progress. Christians must work in the power of the Holy Spirit. We must actively seek to walk in alignment with the Holy Spirit. Sanctification is a partnership between the Christian and the Holy Spirit.

We are to work hard doing all that God commands us to and see it as preparing our sails to catch the wind of the Spirit. When the Holy Spirit blows on and blesses our obedience, there will be real progress in the Christian life. Sanctification will occur. At times it will seem like a mystery, much like the wind does. John 3:8 speaks to this. Our job is patient perseverance in the meantime. The experience of sanctification is often mysterious.

Work and obey from God's love, never for God's love. If you are in Christ, God's love for you is already secured for all eternity. Out of overflow of joy from receiving such love, you should obey. But you are never trying to garner or gain more of his love. You already have it all.

Many parents have experienced the joy of having a young child buy them a present for Christmas. The problem is the child has no money of his own. He may have to ask Dad to take him to the store. He may ask Dad to let him "borrow" twenty dollars. He may ask Dad to wait at the front of the store so the gift can be a surprise.

A good parent delights in the joy the child has over trying to do something to honor and please his parent. But there is no sense of the child spending "his hard-earned money" sacrificially on a gift. The child is literally using Dad's money to buy Dad a gift. This is a great picture of a Christian's obedience.

We can never pay God back for salvation. All we do is go deeper in debt. Because any obedience I ever render him is obedience that he enabled and motivated me to do. Anything good or right that ever happens in or through me is all from him! He gets all the credit, praise, and glory. And yet, God is the ultimate Father. He loves it when his children have a desire to please and honor him. He is delighted when we desire, by grace, to work hard as unto the Lord in the obedience of faith. Every good work a Christian ever does is an outworking of God's ongoing grace in my life.

Application

So, how does one know if you are obeying motivated from love, or if you are obeying to gain God's love? It can be very subtle and gray trying to distinguish your own motives at times. You may be clearly obeying a biblical command. Yet, how can you discern your true motive behind obedience?

The easiest way to tell is how you respond when things do not go your way. I had a friend who had experienced multiple miscarriages and was trying again to get pregnant. I asked if she was praying to get pregnant again. She said no, which was interesting because she worked for a ministry. I asked why not. She essentially said, "What if God doesn't give me a child? I don't know if my heart could handle putting all this time and energy into prayer and then getting nothing for it." I appreciated her honesty but was saddened by the state of her heart.

If any of us are praying for something it makes sense that we will be sad if God says no. But there ought to be a sense of love for and enjoyment of God that drives us to spend time with him in prayer regardless of whether he answers our specific requests or not. We should be so close and intimate with him that we can't help but unburden our hearts before him and tell him all we think, want, and desire. (He already knows all going on in the basement of your heart better than you do! You might as well be ruthlessly honest with him. It'll be freeing, empowering, and liberating when you do! It is one of the ways he practically conforms us to his image.) Jesus commanded us to ask for whatever we desire in places like John 15:7. It is right to do so. In fact, praying the desires of our heart to God would be one specific way to obey the moral law of God. We are commanded to pray. Often God will give us what we want. But how should we respond when, in his infinite wisdom, he decides not to give us what we desire. How will we respond? The answer is telling of our motives.

If you pray fervently for something, do not receive it, and then get angry, it shows you have a legalistic heart at some level. You may not say it out loud, but your attitude and emotions show that you feel you "deserved"

God to give you what you wanted. You feel that you earned it through all your obedience, service, and prayer. But this is misguided.

When any hardship comes in your life how do you respond? Are you like Mrs. Job, who lost all her kids and much of her prosperity, and then her husband got sick? Her response: "Curse God and die!" (Job 2:9b). But Job experienced the same loss as her. Notice his response to the pain of losing all his children and businesses in one day. "The LORD gave and the LORD has taken away. Blessed be the name of the LORD" (Job 1:21b).

Mrs. Job felt she deserved something good from God. Her rationale probably went something like this: "My husband and I are upstanding members of the community. We serve the poor and give lots of money away. We've raised wonderful kids. We honor God with all that we do. How dare God let such tragedy happen to us?! What's the point of all this obedience, if God's not going to bless and protect us from such pain?!" That is a legal spirit.

Job's attitude is clear: "God is good. God is in charge. All good that we have is from God and because of his grace, not because I earned it by obedience. If he chooses to take it away, that too is his right. Whatever the Lord ordains is right. Whatever he does, he is always worthy of my worship and obedience, regardless of if I get what I want or not." Job puts no confidence in the flesh. Neither should we. All our hope and security and sense of self-worth must never come from our deeds or efforts, but only from the God of grace above.

Most Christians wonder at some point why a good God would ever let painful things happen to his saved children. It is an understandable question. At least one reason is a trial to expose our hearts' motives to ourselves so that we can more fully repent of any legalism and more deeply trust in him alone.

Conclusion

The following illustration has helped me live in the tension of taking obedience seriously but always being motivated by grace to obey. Imagine you are in the cosmic courtroom of the universe. You are the defendant charged with breaking the Ten Commandments. You know you are guilty. God the Father is the Judge, sitting behind the bench.

The Lord Jesus Christ comes in as your defense attorney. He looks at you and says, "Don't worry, I'll handle this." You respond, "But I am guilty and deserve death based on God's moral law!" He says with a smile, "I know, but the Judge is my dad. I'm going to save you not based on your performance, which is rotten, but based on my own performance, which is perfect. And trust me. I know my Father's heart perfectly. He is totally aligned with my desire to save you. We planned this whole thing together!"

Then Jesus addresses his Father. "Father, I lived and died and rose as a saving sacrifice for this one. He must go free." The Father responds with joy, "You are right, my Son." The gavel falls, and the Father declares, "The defendant is justified! Not guilty! Case closed!"

You stand, stunned beyond belief. The Father leaves the bench and takes off his judge's robe and hangs it on the wall. He doesn't walk out of the back of the courtroom as we often see in a trial. Rather, he walks over to you and puts his arm around you. He says, "I heard in that trial that you used to be a child of Satan (John 8:44). But now you are free from him, so in a sense you are an orphan. Well, I'd like to adopt you into my family." You can only nod your head in the affirmative, still too stunned to speak. The Father puts his arm around you and says, "Great! Right this way." He walks you across the street to a mansion so large you cannot even see the whole thing. He walks you inside.

He begins to give you the tour of the home. He introduces you to your new adopted family. He says, "What's mine is yours" as he shows you the different rooms and food and provisions the house contains. As you walk through the living room, you see the Ten Commandments written down, hanging over the mantel on the wall. You begin to tremble in fear and point, "What are those? Why are they here?"

The Father responds warmly, "Those are the family rules."

You ask in trepidation, "What does that mean?"

The Father answers, "Well, those explain what I am like. Those laws explain what I love. If you live here, you must agree to obey them."

You shudder in fear and terror. "But I've tried to keep them before, and I failed miserably! I can't do it! What happens if I break them?!"

The Father looks concerned and serious. "Well, if you blatantly disobey me there will be consequences. You may have to go to bed with no dinner or something like that. We will see. I love you so much and I know obeying my law is what is best for you. I am willing to bring some small, short-term pain into your life to help you stay on the best path. But also, now my Spirit lives in you and will help you grow in obedience, slowly but surely."

You still don't fully understand and just shake your head in silence. The Father perfectly understands your concern and speaks tenderly to you. "My child do not worry or fear. I will fill you with my Spirit to help you obey. You won't be able to perfectly obey in this life, but you will grow. And if you disobey there will be discipline and fatherly chastisement. But here is what I promise. You will always be my child. I will discipline you in love like a child. I will never take you back across the street to the courtroom. I will never wear my judicial robe again when I interact with you. Those days are over. From now on, I am your adopted Father by grace! Live and enjoy your new life in Christ!"

God is good. God is Savior. Enjoy his salvation. Relish your adoption in Christ. And then, out of the overflow of love, joy, and gratitude, seek to obey and please the lover of your soul!

Conclusion

IMAGINE TWO SISTERS WHO both get married to terrible husbands. Their husbands are both mean, angry, abusive men. They beat the women. They do all they can to control their wives and keep them under their thumb.

The two sisters respond radically differently. The older sister tries her best to please her husband. She assumes she must not be a good enough wife. She tries to serve him and obey him as best she can. But it is never enough. Nothing she can do ever seems to help or appease him.

The younger sister is totally opposite. She rebels. She fights back. She lies. She sneaks out. She has multiple affairs. She openly hates her husband, understandably so.

Then, both of their husbands die, and thus both sisters are free of the abusive men. There is an initial sense of joy, freedom, and relief. But it doesn't last long.

Later, two other men come along and propose marriage. Both widows are understandably nervous. Their first marriages were so bad and traumatic. They are hesitant to try again.

The older sister cannot stand the thought of trying so hard to please an impossible "lover." The younger sister is sick and tired of having to sneak around and rebel to be herself and find joy in her life. Both initially refuse the proposals.

But both suitors persist. One of the women eventually says yes, with much fear and trepidation. But she finds this relationship radically different than her first marriage.

Her new husband is kind, patient, warm, inviting, gentle, and understanding. Much more importantly, he is forgiving when she fails. He does not beat his wife for her imperfections. He helps her. He is tender and affectionate. He genuinely loves her. She begins to blossom, not only as a wife, but as a human being in every way.

The married sister one day talks to her sister who has chosen to stay single. The single woman asks, "How could you ever willingly submit to marriage again? It is such an evil, tyrannical institution." Her married sister responds, "There is nothing wrong with marriage. Marriage done rightly is wonderful beyond imagination. The wrong was in the husband who held the power in our marriage." With this reasoning, slowly but surely, she persuades her sister to get married again to a more gracious man.

We come into this world under the covenant of works. The moral law of God reigns supreme over us whether we like it or not. It demands perfection. It is written on our hearts. Our consciences alternately accuse and defend us. But overall, we are condemned, rightly so because of our indwelling sin. It is easy to come to hate the law. Further, we can despise the one who wrote the law. We can hate the glorious lawgiver in our wickedness.

But God became man to seek and save the lost. Christ fulfilled the law perfectly for his people. He died under the curse of the law we all had earned. When we trust in Christ for salvation, we are forever free from the covenant of works. We are free from relating to the law as a covenant. The law is now our counsel on how we should live to honor and please the lover of our souls, our Savior.

Just as marriage was not the problem for the women, the law is not our problem. An evil husband was the problem for the women in their first marriages. Sin and Satan are our real problems. When sin uses the law to arouse sin in us as Rom 7 teaches, we can understandably come to hate the law. When the law condemns us rightfully for our sin, we may tremble in fear and trepidation.

But when Christ, as our Savior and the husband of our souls, is the one holding the power of the law in our lives, his yoke is easy, and his burden is light (Matt 11:30). He uses the law to guide us, not to condemn us. He uses the law to strengthen and mature us, not to shame us.

When we receive the law directly from Moses alone with no grace, it falls on us with an impossibly heavy burden. When we receive the law from our gracious Savior and husband, Christ, it is a helpful blessing. If we are in Christ, we are no longer children of Satan. We are not married to the law. We are married to Christ. We have no cause to fear the law anymore.

We may have had terrible experiences of the law before we were Christians. We may have had terrible experiences when we were immature Christians and did not understand what the Bible teaches about the role of the law in the covenant of grace. We may have been led into a legalism that strove to please God in our own strength, which is obviously impossible. This can leave us tired and weary and terrified of ever trying to obey again.

We may have been led into an antinomian spirit that sought to throw off all the law's demands as suffocating. The thought of once again submitting to the law is stifling. It seems impossible. But we must remember we are now empowered by the Holy Spirit to slowly but surely, by grace, fulfill the law in this life. We can be gloriously conformed to the image of Christ, even now. We will not be fully glorified until the next life, but the process truly starts at the moment of regeneration.

If I think that it is all my effort and all my strength alone that produces my sanctification, I am a legalist. If I believe that is all God's work and all his energy alone that produces my growth, I will be licentious. If I believe that I partner with the indwelling Holy Spirit to walk in a manner worthy of the Lord, I will be a wise, growing believer (Col 1:10). If I know and am assured that I must put in 100 percent effort, even while the Holy Spirit brings all the power of enabling me to change and grow in his grace, I will be following the moral law in just the way the Lord has always intended. "I labor, striving according to his power, which mightily works within me (Col 1:29).

God is good. God is Savior. Enjoy his free salvation. Relish your adoption in Christ. And then, out of overflow of love, joy, and gratitude . . . *trust and obey*!

Glossary

THIS GLOSSARY IS PROVIDED to help readers understand how some terms are used in this book.

Adamic covenant—The covenant God made in the garden of Eden with Adam in Gen 2. It is also called the covenant of works or of law or of life. The bottom line was Adam had to obey God's commands to earn his right to stay in the garden and to remain in loving relationship with God. Adam failed. Because all people are descended from Adam, we are all born into the Adamic covenant as lawbreakers. We are all born dead in our sins. We can never be saved through the covenant of works because it demands moral perfection and none of us can attain that in this life.

Antinomianism—This is a lawless way of life. Antinomians believe that the moral law does not apply to them in any significant fashion, either because God and or his law do not exist, or because they are saved by grace alone and thus free from the need or obligation to obey in any way in this life.

Ceremonial law—God's specific application of the moral law for ancient Israel under the Mosaic covenant before Christ came, pertaining to worship. It regulated their worship practices. It told them practically how to love God in that day and age and setting.

Civil law—God's specific application of the moral law for ancient Israel under the Mosaic covenant before Christ came, pertaining to loving neighbors. It regulated their interactions with other human beings. It taught them practically how to love one another in that day and age and setting.

Covenant—A biblical covenant is a unique, unilateral, solemn relationship between God and man with significant conditions and/or implications.

Covenant of creation—This is synonymous with the Adamic covenant. See above.

Covenant of grace—The covenant of grace is first introduced in Gen 3:15. It is God's plan of salvation for all his people in the Old and New Testament times. Christ fulfilled the moral law in our place and died to pay the price for our sins. If anyone trusts in Christ alone for salvation and not their own works, they will be saved by grace alone. This was true for all who lived before Christ's resurrection, as they looked forward to God's promise of a coming Messiah. This is true for all who live after Christ's resurrection who look back to a risen Savior.

Covenant of life—This is synonymous with the Adamic covenant. See above.

Covenant of works—This is synonymous with the Adamic covenant. See above.

Justification—God's once-and-for-all free gift to his people whereby they are declared legally righteous because of the righteousness of Christ, credited for them.

Law of Christ—The moral law of God coming to his people from Christ and the New Testament in the covenant of grace.

Legalism—The belief that what a person does can earn them something good in their relationship with God, whether that be salvation or other blessings.

Libertinism—This is synonymous with antinomianism. See above.

Licentiousness—This is synonymous with antinomianism. See above.

Moral law—God's rules for all people, at all times, in all places. These laws are written on all human hearts, meaning all people have some instinctual knowledge of them even if it is dim and unclear. God's law was summarized in the Old Testament in the Ten Commandments and summarized by Jesus in the New Testament in the two great commandments, love God and love your neighbor.

Mosaic covenant—The covenant God made with Moses and the nation of Israel in the book of Exodus. God's people, the nation of Israel—the church in the Old Testament times—lived under the Mosaic covenant from the time of Moses until the time of Christ. The Mosaic covenant was governed by the Mosaic law. The Mosaic covenant is ultimately an extension of the covenant of grace, even though it highlighted the covenant of works.

Mosaic law—The Mosaic law was the law of God given to Moses and recorded in Exodus, Leviticus, Numbers, and Deuteronomy. It contains three main parts: the moral, the ceremonial, and the civil. The moral is still authoritative today. The ceremonial and civil are no longer binding.

Old covenant—The Old Testament. God's way of working with his people before the coming of Christ. This includes the Mosaic covenant. This was the ancient expression of the covenant of grace.

New covenant—The New Testament. God's way of working with his people since the coming of Christ. This is the present expression of and experience of the covenant of grace.

Bibliography

Augustine. *The City of God*. Translated by Marcus Dods. New York: Random House, 1993.

Baldwin, Joyce G. *Genesis 12–50*. Downers Grove, IL: InterVarsity, 1986.

Bolton, Samuel. *The True Bounds of Christian Freedom*. Carlisle, PA: Banner of Truth, 2001.

Bray, Gerald, ed. *Galatians, Ephesians*. Reformation Commentary on Scripture: New Testament 10. Downers Grove, IL: IVP Academic, 2011.

Brooks, Thomas. *Precious Remedies Against Satan's Devices*. Carlisle, PA: Banner of Truth, 2000.

Brueggemann, Walter. *Genesis*. Louisville: Westminster John Knox, 2010.

Bunyan, John. *Pilgrim's Progress*. Petersburg, KY: Answers in Genesis, 2006.

Calvin, John. *Commentaries on the Epistle of Paul the Apostle to the Romans*. Translated and edited by John Owen. Grand Rapids: Baker, 2003.

———. *Commentaries on the Epistles of Paul the Apostle to the Galatians and Ephesians*. Translated and edited by John Owen. Grand Rapids: Baker, 2003.

———. *Harmony of the Evangelists*. Vol. 2. Grand Rapids: Baker, 2003.

Carson, D. A. *Matthew Chapters 1 Through 12*. Grand Rapids: Zondervan, 1995.

Crowe, Brandon D. *The Path of Faith*. Downers Grove, IL: InterVarsity, 2021.

DeYoung, Kevin. *The Good News We Almost Forgot*. Chicago: Moody, 2010.

Ferguson, Sinclair. *The Christian Life*. Carlisle, PA: Banner of Truth, 2023.

———. *The Whole Christ*. Wheaton, IL: Crossway, 2016.

Fisher, Edward. *The Marrow of Modern Divinity*. Ross-shire, UK: Christian Focus, 2009.

Hall, Elvina M. "Jesus Paid It All." *The Hymnal for Worship and Celebration*, 210. Waco, TX: Word Music, 1986.

Hendriksen, William. *Luke*. Grand Rapids: Baker, 2002.

———. *Matthew*. Grand Rapids: Baker, 2002.

Henry, Matthew. *The NIV Matthew Henry Commentary*. Grand Rapids: Zondervan, 1992.

Keller, Tim. *Romans*. New York: Redeemer, 2003.

Koukl, Greg. "Telling Parting Words." Stand to Reason. Feb. 1, 2019. https://www.str.org/w/telling-parting-words-john-newton-vs-mr-rogers.

Luther, Martin. *Commentary on Galatians*. Modern English Edition. Grand Rapids: Revell, 1999.

Murray, John. *The Epistle to the Romans*. Grand Rapids: Eerdmans, 1997.

Owen, John. *Glory of Christ*. Ross-shire, UK: Christian Focus, 2004.

———. *Sin and Temptation*. Minneapolis: Bethany, 1996.

Parish, Shane. "The Munger Operating System: How to Live a Life That Really Works." FS. https://fs.blog/munger-operating-system/.

Perkins, William. *The Art of Prophesying.* Carlisle, PA: Banner of Truth, 1982.

Piper, John. "Why Is Witchcraft Handled So Differently Across Scripture?" Desiring God, Feb. 6, 2025. https://www.desiringgod.org/interviews/why-is-witchcraft-handled-so-differently-across-scripture.

Poole, Matthew. *Matthew Poole's Commentary on the Holy Bible.* Vol. 3. Peabody, MA: Hendrickson, 1985.

Presbyterian Church (U.S.A.). *The Constitution of the Presbyterian Church.* Pt. 1, *The Book of Confessions.* Atlanta: Office of the General Assembly, 1983.

Rowell, Amy. "Thank God I'm Not a Gentile, a Woman, or a Slave." City Church, Nov. 9, 2020. https://citychurchmpls.org/bible-devotionals/thank-god-im-not-a-gentile-a-woman-or-a-slave/.

Sibbes, Richard. *The Bruised Reed.* Carlisle, PA: Banner of Truth, 1998.

Sproul, R. C. "What Does 'Simul Justus et Peccator' Mean?" Ligonier Updates, Oct. 17, 2019. https://www.ligonier.org/posts/simul-justus-et-peccator.

Stapleton, Chris. "You Should Probably Leave." *Starting Over.* Mercury Nashville, 2020. Apple iTunes.

Stott, John. *The Letters of John.* Downers Grove, IL: InterVarsity, 1988.

———. *Men Made New.* Grand Rapids: Baker, 1987.

———. *Romans.* Downers Grove, IL: InterVarsity, 1994.

Stubbs, Olan. "Law and Covenant." Sermon series. *Truth Wars* (podcast), 2024. https://gospeltalk.podbean.com/category/law-and-covenant.

Ward, Rowald S., ed. *The Westminster Confession and Catechisms in Modern English.* Victoria: New Melbourne, 2000.

Wesley, Charles. "And Can It Be?" In *The Hymnal for Worship and Celebration*, 203. Waco, TX: Word Music, 1986.

www.ingramcontent.com/pod-product-compliance
Lightning Source LLC
LaVergne TN
LVHW050649100826
845148LV00011B/2047

* 9 7 9 8 3 8 5 2 7 0 5 6 9 *